"The relinquishment experience, the shame and grief that Beth Kane describes so well in this book, will resonate with all birthmothers. This book speaks for a generation of birthmothers who have not yet 'come out' in force to be heard and supported. It will help them shed their own fears and revel in reconnecting with their 'lost' children. Beth's instant and loving response to her son will touch and open many hearts."

Birthmother Merrill Clarke Hunn, Board Member and support group facilitator for Post Adoption Center for Education and Research (PACER) Mill Valley, CA

"What a privilege to read a first copy of this book. As an adoptive mother it made the tears flow and made me wish that Beth could have been the birthmother of one of my three adult children. Once I started to read the book I couldn't put it down."

Adoptive Mother Jane Limb-Brown, San Marcos, CA

"As an adoptee who has been through the search and reunion process, I really didn't know how heart-rendering it must have been for a birthmother to make her decision with the best interest of the child in mind. I had always incorrectly assumed that I just wasn't wanted . . . an inconvenience. This book is a must read for adoptees."

Adoptee   Society
(Adult

"Beth   up her
son fo   united
with   story."

Helen

"Beth   understand   7."

Louis   riter

BAKER & TAYLOR

Thank You, Son, for Finding Me

Thank You, Son, for Finding Me

A Birthmother's Story

Beth J. Kane

Aslan Publishing
Fairfield, Connecticut

Aslan Publishing
2490 Black Rock Turnpike, Suite 342
Fairfield, CT 06432
(203) 372-0300
FAX (203) 374-4766
E-mail info@aslanpublishing.com

For a free catalog of our other titles, or to order more copies of this book please call (800) 786-5427 or visit our website at www.aslanpublishing.com.

© 1999 by Beth Kane

Library of Congress Cataloging-in-Publication Data

Kane, Beth J., 1927–
    Thank you son for finding me : a birthmother's story/by Beth J. Kane.
        p. cm.
    ISBN 0-944031-82-X (pbk. : alk. paper)
    1. Kane, Beth J., 1927– . 2. Birthmothers—United States Biography.
3. Adoption—United States Case studies. 4. Birthmothers—United
States—Identification Case studies. 5. Mothers and sons—United States
Case studies. I. Title.
HV874.82.K36A3 1999
362.82′98′092–dc21
  [B]   99-24879
                                                 CIP

Cover and book design by Sans Serif Inc., Saline, Michigan
Edited by Chuck Cordova, Marcia Yudkin, Barbara H. Levine
Printed in USA by Baker Johnson Inc., Dexter, Michigan

Aslan Publishing—Our Mission

Aslan Publishing offers readers a window to the soul via well-crafted and practical self-help books, inspirational books and modern day parables. Our mission is to publish books that uplift one's mind, body and spirit.

Living one's spirituality in business, relationships, and personal growth is the underlying purpose of our publishing company, and the meaning behind our name Aslan Publishing. We see the word "Aslan" as a metaphor for living spiritually in a physical world.

Aslan means "lion" in several Middle Eastern languages. The most famous "Aslan" is a lion in *The Chronicles of Narnia* by C. S. Lewis. In these stories, Aslan is the Messiah, the One who appears at critical points in the story in order to point human beings in the right direction. Aslan doesn't preach, he acts. His actions are an inherent expression of who he is.

We hope to point the way toward joyful, satisfying and healthy relationships with oneself and with others. Our purpose is to make a real difference in the everyday lives of our readers.

Barbara H. Levine   Harold Levine

To God, for being there for me.
To Mother Nature, for creating the magnetic force of the bond between mother and child. To my son's adoptive parents for giving him the love and life he deserved, then to Susan, for whispering in her brother's ear from Heaven, "Find Mom!"

TABLE OF CONTENTS

ACKNOWLEDGMENTS

First and foremost, I wish to thank my son, Mike Dobbins. His long search and finding me opened the door to my past, causing me to remember in order to tell him our story through writing this book. Thanks to my great husband, Chuck, for his love for me and the pure joy I feel of his acceptance of Mike. Thank you too for the way he helped me through many unusual and awkward situations. Thanks to our daughter Linda, for being the special daughter that she is and for her delight in knowing her brother and her encouragement to me to write this book. A very special thanks for the love and support from all my grandchildren, Linda's daughter Guinevere and Susan's two children, Stephanie and Gregory. Thanks now to Mike's two daughters, Kim and Seana as well, who never lost hope and had fun watching me.

My special thanks to Vicki Quinn, an adoptee, Jane Limb-Brown, an adoptive mother, and Merrill Hunn a birthmother. These women, all members of the adoption triad, contributed greatly to my knowledge.

Thanks to Phyllis Fox, who edits for my son's newspaper, THE WILDWOOD INDEPENDENT, and was the first professional to read my book. She pointed out the similarities my son and I share in our style of writing.

Thanks to the mother and daughter team, Dorothy M. Scheflo, owner of "Mail Boxes, Etc." and her daughter Karen Scheflo, in Stockton, California. Dorothy and Karen have been involved through each mailing and remailing, and never once lost their resolve that I should not give up.

Thank you to Barbara Levine, the publisher from Aslan Publishing, for her first phone call after reading three chapters and wanting to read more. Thanks to her and her husband Hal for their faith in my story. I understand it was Marcia Yudkin who first read my manuscript and had enthusiasm for the story, I thank her much for her reaction. And then there is the editor, Chuck Cordova who taught me a lot about using words. It was actually fun working with him.

I have met many friends in our Stockton, California, Adult Liberty Movement Association (ALMA) Chapter. Vicki Quinn, our leader, Pam Abare and Joan Southwick and I were a great team as we were helping others to find their loved ones.

Thanks to all the women I have met from PACER (Post Adoption Center For Education & Research), for all the support they provide around the San Francisco Bay Area. These women are friends now and I want to thank them for their respect and enthusiasm for my writing this book. There's Jane Calbreath, President; Merrill Hunn, and Laura Ingram, who have made me feel safe while in the throes of the emotional impact of our reunion. PACER provides all the members of the adoption triad a safe haven to tell their stories. Thanks to the AAC (American Adoption Congress) for offering all the educational information and working hard to change the law for open birth records so that every adoptee can know who he/she is and where he/she came from.

And last but certainly not least, thank you to THE AUTUMN WRITERS, of Stockton, California, my writers' group. This wonderful group of people, writers all, have been with me through every step of the creation of my book. Without their push and support, would I have stuck with it? They are

Joe Drovdal, Jack Stewart, George Davies, Mo Hackett, Louise Bartholomew, Gev Bonato, Gloria David, Betti Honer and Perky Peling. This group of dynamic oldies have proven that one can learn to write and have fun. Special thanks to Betti Honer for her help through a very hard rewrite.

And my very special thanks to my mentor and good friend, Perky Peling, who painstakingly went over each word as a whiz-bang grammar expert. Her advice and input is beyond description. She was always there every time I panicked over something while writing the proposal. With her soothing calming voice, saying, "Sure, bring it over and we can take a look at what you have done." Thank you, Perky, for all your encouragement.

Beth Kane
Stockton, CA.

FOREWORD

When I proposed marriage to my wife Beth in 1949, she told me a deep secret which only a tiny group of people shared. In 1947, she had borne a son out of wedlock and placed him for adoption.

Through all our years of marriage we spoke very little about her secret. The only thoughts shared were on his birthdays and the worry of harm to him during the Vietnam War as he was the right age.

When our two daughters became young ladies, Beth shared her secret with them. Even our closest friends remained unaware of Beth's secret.

From that day in 1993 when Beth's son Mike found us and introduced himself, I have watched and learned. I had been taught that environment is the primary influence in human development, and heredity has little effect. Now that seems incorrect. To me, Mike is a reincarnation of a man he never knew, Beth's older brother Bill, my fishing buddy. Some of our friends remark how Mike looks like Beth's family, and his daughters look, and sometimes act, like our two girls.

But the real change is with Beth. I now believe the loss of her son affected her all those years without her really knowing it. Mike is no longer a secret.

Of course, both Beth and I know that Mike's real parents are the mother and father who adopted him and made him the person he is today.

My new buddy, Mike is a lot more than a friend to Beth.

As you read my wife's story I believe you will learn as I did that Adoptees, Adopting Parents, and Birth-parents—all the people involved in the adoption process should be considered and understood.

Charles Kane

1

SPECIAL DELIVERY LETTER

'm sitting in this dark car not knowing what to expect. Taking a deep breath and looking around the parking lot, I'm relieved to see it's well lighted. Sighing, I nervously look at the clock on the dash. Good. I still have a few minutes before nine.

When he arrives and I have to get out of the car, we should be able to get a good look at each other. Thinking about that makes my heart pound and I can feel my whole body tremble. Chuck puts his arm around my shoulders and tells me not to worry.

"Beth, it will all work out."

"I can't believe I'm sitting here waiting for this to happen," I respond.

Feeling suspended in time, I tell my husband, "I'm glad you're here." My mind tells me over and over that I'm waiting to meet a person I have never seen before—a person who has had a major effect on my life.

Will I be able to handle this? What if he has made a mistake? What will happen when he sees me? He could be very angry for what I did to him. How is it possible that only seven hours ago I was a different person, living in a different world?

In that world, it was just another hot August day. Chuck and I were still sitting over lunch at two o'clock, watching CNN. We were just whiling the time away. The pace of our life was proving to be anything but on the fast track. Both in our sixties and not doing much of anything, we were finding it hard to think like retired people. We were bored, very bored.

Since moving to Stockton, California a few years earlier, we had not been able to feel settled or get a sense of direction. The last three years had been busy with our ill and dying parents. And the loss of one of our daughters eight years earlier had been the reason we left the Bay Area—too many painful memories.

Chuck and I have a good life. We are well traveled, look good and are in good health. We had two beautiful daughters and have three wonderful grandchildren who are healthy, bright and happy. We have a nice home and nice things, nice everything. In fact, we are the envy of our friends. Then why were we feeling so loose and disconnected?

Feeling the need to find a satisfying way to fill the next twenty years, my constant lament was, "I've got to get started on whatever will happen next." I was always living in the past or worrying about an empty future, never living in the present. I was forever talking about writing a book about our daughter, Susan, to tell of her two-year battle with brain cancer—how we all pitched in to try to save her life, how she managed to carry on as a mother to her children despite the trauma of her year of chemotherapy.

She worked hard to put us at ease with her illness, and with her inner strength and positive attitude she was with us a year and a half longer than the doctors had expected. It's a beautiful story, and I need the world to know about her. But all I do is talk. I can't get over the feeling of melancholy and a sense of emptiness.

I have accepted this sadness as the way it will be from now on and I am living with it. After all, aren't I the expert on grieving, reading every book on the subject? In fact, the first year after her death, I made a career of learning all about grief so I could get through the loss of her with my sanity still intact. But the feeling would not go away.

When the doorbell rang, we were both startled. Who could it be? Chuck and I got up at the same time to answer, like children wanting to be the first to see who was there. Reaching the door first, I opened it quickly and was surprised to see the mailman.

"Wow, a Special Delivery letter for me," I exclaimed.

The letter was in a plain white envelope. Chuck was leaning over my shoulder and saying, "What is it? Who's it from?"

"Wait a minute!" I said as I signed for it. Having to sign for a letter made me think someone was going to great lengths to sell us something. We were both excited and I sensed that Chuck would try to grab the letter from me.

"Hey," I said as I avoided his reaching hand, "it's addressed to me."

"Who is it from?" he repeated.

As we walked back to the kitchen, I told him, "I don't know yet. Give me a chance to open it. It's from Nevada City. Who do we know in Nevada City?"

—"No one," I answered myself, carefully opening the envelope. "It's probably an advertisement, but who would send an advertisement Special Delivery?"

The envelope held two typed pages.

"Who's it from? See who signed it," Chuck was saying as I looked at the signatures.

Still standing in the kitchen, I answered, "Mike and John from Nevada City. I don't have any idea who Mike and John from Nevada City could be." Anxious and ignoring the lunch dishes, I joined Chuck and sat down to read the letter out loud.

3

"Dear Beth," it started. "Please accept my apologies for the method by which this was delivered to you. As will soon become apparent, my nervousness over this missive, and its impact, left me little recourse but to make sure it was handed to you personally."

I looked at Chuck and said, "I don't get this. It doesn't sound right."

"My name is Mike Dobbins," the letter went on. "That name will mean nothing to you. However, for the first three months of my life, my name was John Heath."

I stopped reading.

"Someone is playing a cruel hoax."

I felt that a ghost from the past had found out about me. I wondered what they were after. As I continued to read, my heart started pounding.

"I hope that name *does* mean something to you," the letter went on. "If it doesn't, then please forgive this intrusion and discard the rest of this letter."

I couldn't believe what I was reading. They had my name right, my parents' names right—all the information was correct. I couldn't look at Chuck.

"What is going on here?" I asked, and had the fleeting thought that someone was throwing my past in my face. Then I said, "Someone went to a lot of trouble trying to sell us something."

I was waiting for a punch line of some sort, maybe even a chain letter. Or perhaps a threat of exposure?

I continued to read out loud.

"If that is you, Hi, Mom!"

I gasped and my throat constricted. I could hardly speak.

"It's been a rather long search, fraught with fear and uncertainty but also exciting and now very rewarding."

My eyes glazed over and it was difficult to see the typed pages. I could hear my heart pounding. My mind cried out, *Oh, my God! This can't be true! Hi, Mom? It can't be him!*

4

After so many years—forty-five years, to be exact—and he sent this letter, he found me, now!

Chuck knew I had a child before we met. Feeling I had to be honest with him, I had told him about my son before he asked me to marry him. I remember thinking at the time (in 1949) that he might not want to marry me—a woman who had a child out of wedlock. Feeling unreal, I knew when the letter mentioned Henry's last name with the correct spelling that the letter was genuine. Henry was the name of his father. With my heart sinking, I thought, *What are they after?*

My child, whom I had given up for adoption in 1947, was alive! Not able to believe all this, I was dumbfounded. He's alive and he has found me! I sat there numb and looked at Chuck, not knowing what to expect. He had the most incredible smile on his face. With a sob in my throat, I sighed in relief.

He said, "Call him, call him right now!"

"No, I can't. I don't believe this!"

This can't be happening, I kept thinking. *It can't be true.* The totally unexpected shock was beyond words. Taking a deep breath, I continued to read.

"This letter is written not to disrupt or threaten you, but merely to reach out and say Hi."

They went on to tell me that they live only two hours from our front door.

"It was a shock to find you so close after scouring the country, checking out every Beth, Betty and Elizabeth Heath, later Kane (there are a lot!)."

I was beginning to feel less threatened as the letter told me, "The people to whom you entrusted my care and upbringing did a fine job, providing a loving and nurturing environment. My parents live close by and are enjoying retirement."

This Mike or John, whoever, sounded like a good person who had put his heart into this letter. He sounded nice, not angry. Confused, I decided to look at the signatures again. I saw that it was signed Mike *nee* John, not Mike and John. Now it all made sense.

I stopped reading the letter at this point and thought about what Mike had just told me. He'd had a good childhood and good parents. Thank God! I was overwhelmed with feelings I had never had before. Knowing he'd had a good life, I experienced my first sense of relief. Oh, my God! What if his life had been terrible? What would I do? I wouldn't be able to do anything. The thought was horrible.

He next said, "I'd like you to know you have two incredibly beautiful granddaughters, Kim, 25, and Seana, 21."

"Beth," Chuck said, "you have two more granddaughters. Imagine you being the grandmother of a twenty-five-year-old. I can't wait to meet them. Keep reading."

I just couldn't grasp the enormity of having two more grandchildren. Two more girls! This was too wonderful for words. As I continued to read, I discovered that Mike had been a police officer for the first ten years of his adult life. I looked at Chuck, amazed. Chuck, a retired law enforcement officer, shook his head in wonder. Already they had something in common.

Mike went on to say, "After an on-the-job injury shortened that career, I moved to Northern California where, for the past sixteen years, I've been a journalist, most recently working as a correspondent for a local newspaper."

"He was a policeman, Chuck! My God! And now he's a writer in the newspaper business!"

"That's great," Chuck said, still in disbelief.

The coincidence that Mike had been in law enforcement, as Chuck had been, was astounding. Mike could have been anything, but to have been a police officer! I finished reading the letter, then I just sat there and stared into space. Mike's letter said that through his search he discovered that his father had died in 1969, at the age of forty-five, and he hoped to learn the cause of his death for medical reasons. I felt sorry that Henry had died so young.

6

"Beth," Chuck said full of excitement, "two more grand-daughters, and your son has found you." After taking a deep breath, he again insisted, "Call that phone number right now. He's probably anxious and waiting."

"I can't, Chuck. Give me time to get my head together. I'm afraid to believe all this."

I reread the letter many times, trying to determine what kind of a person had written it. I found this person to be sensitive and warm—at least the letter was. I asked myself, "How could it be that the baby I gave birth to and never laid eyes on actually wrote this letter to me? But here it is, right here in front of me. I'm looking at it."

I had absolutely buried all of that when I had walked away from him. After forty-five years without a son, how was it possible that he is here? I couldn't believe it, or take it all in. It was all too good to be true. Suddenly I couldn't sit still. I got up and paced back and forth, taking deep breaths.

I felt exposed. But why? The past was buried. A long-ago event. An event that was very traumatic and buried deep in my heart. Now a feeling of happiness was trying to surface, but I was afraid to let it happen. What if it wasn't real?

Remembering our daughter, I said, "Linda! I have to tell Linda!"

Chuck, still sitting there watching me, smiled.

"Yes," he said, "call her."

2

FOUND THE RIGHT PERSON

Trembling, I couldn't remember Linda's number; I had to try three times. What a surprise this would be for her. Living in California's Wine Country, she wasn't too far away.

"Hi, Linda, are you sitting down?" I started.

"No. Should I?"

"I think you'd better." I quickly added, "I have big news, nothing bad. You're not going to believe what happened."

"What? Tell me."

"I just received a Special Delivery letter, and. . . ." I was losing my breath. "And it's from. . . ."

I couldn't say the word, so Linda said it for me.

"Your son? Mom! How wonderful!"

Her voice told me how delighted she was, and surprised. How could she know? Was it something in my voice? Maybe, I thought, she knew because a few months ago I had spent a week visiting her, and while there a friend of Linda's, who is a birth-mother, was found by her daughter.

Perhaps it was fresh in Linda's mind. It flashed before me, while on the phone, the scene at Linda's the day Linda's friend had met her daughter for the first time. We had celebrated and shared her happiness. She had told us she knew her daughter was coming to visit her, and when she opened her living room door, she saw a taller version of herself standing there, holding pink streamers and a bright silver balloon that said, "It's a Girl!"

Looking at their pictures, we couldn't believe the resemblance between mother and daughter. I found myself telling Linda's friend about my son. I can remember thinking at the time how strange it was feeling happy for her and yet not feeling envious. I could not imagine that ever happening to me; it was absolutely out of the question.

Linda and Susan knew about my son; I had told them when they were in their teens. Thank God! But naturally it wasn't something we talked about much.

"Linda! Guess what else?" I continued. "Mike's wife is a Linda too."

"You're kidding," was all she could answer. Then she said, "Mother, read the letter to me."

I read to her that Mike's daughter, Kim, had graduated from college last May and his other daughter, Seana, would graduate next May.

Linda said, "College, how great!"

As I continued, the letter went on to say that Mike's wife, Linda, and Kim and Seana had all encouraged and supported him when he began to lose hope. They had not wanted him to give up. He had written, "I'm very lucky to have them on my side."

Then I read to Linda, "It's important for me to tell you that I did not become an ax murderer, rapist, or child molester."

I said, "Think about that, Linda. He's okay and a good person, and he really wants me to know that."

"Mom," Linda commented, "I can see that he would want you to know that right away."

"Gosh," I said, worried, "he has no idea what he will find in me."

9

"Oh, Mother, don't be ridiculous. You're great!"

Mike's letter went on to tell me about himself, his career, his interest in the arts and history, and his passion for golf. In high school and college he had been active in sports, as I had been at that age. When I read to Linda that Mike had been a policeman for ten years, her reply was, with a chuckle, "What, another cop in the family? What a coincidence, two cops and two Lindas."

Mike's letter continued, "I would very much like to communicate with you on some level. From what I've been able to glean, you're someone I'd very much like to know better."

"Linda," I said, "he wants to know me. Can this be happening?"

"It's real, Mom; he sounds nice. The letter really tells a lot about him."

I read on.

"It is my sincere hope not to cause you any discomfort. You can call me anytime. Or write, or send a fax! ANYTHING!"

His closing thought was, "If you can't, please at least respond to this letter and let me know you read this. I will be anxious for any reply."

"Mom, this is great!" Linda said. "Call him right now!"

We went over the letter several times, analyzing every word, every nuance. Reading between the lines, we determined that Mike seemed able to express his emotions well. He'd had a good life and childhood. His adoptive parents were nice people and had raised him well. He felt it important for me to know that. Linda and I found it touching and thoughtful. The more we talked about him, the more interesting he seemed and the more excited we were to meet him.

"Mom, I'm happy for you," Linda said, "and for me, too. It couldn't have happened at a better time in your life and Dad's." She rushed on to say, "Call him soon, try to get together as soon as possible. Let me know. Mom, I love you and I'm thrilled for you."

Sitting in our patio, while talking to Linda on the phone and looking around our garden, I was struck by its beauty. There was a new brilliance to it, the bright color of the flowers, the green of the trees. Even the sky was brighter and bluer. Had everything been this beautiful yesterday? Something was happening to me. Everything looked clean and pure.

Chuck kept urging me to make the call. He came to the patio door and said, "It sounds like Linda is very happy about this. She has a brother. Beth, you should call him right now."

I picked up the phone, started to punch in his number, then put the phone down. *What would I say? How would he feel about me?* Although frantic, I placed the call and waited. When I heard a voice on the answering machine, I quickly hung up.

I couldn't leave a message. What on earth would I say? After pacing the floor and having a flood of long-buried memories, I felt my anxieties mounting. I told myself, *It's time to call again.* No answer, again, but this time I decided to leave a message. I took a deep breath and told the voice on the answering machine, "Hello, I'm sitting here looking at a Special Delivery letter."

I told him my name, my maiden name, the names of my parents, and then I said, "You have found the right person."

I went on to say how I felt about receiving the letter: shocked, excited, frightened, happy, thrilled and on and on, until his tape ran out. I had talked too much, so I hung up, embarrassed. However, I had a chance to say, "I definitely would like to meet you."

I wandered around the house in a daze. Chuck was delighted, and I was thankful because this could have been a very awkward situation. We have been through so much together over the years. He told me, with a happy look on his face, "I've thought about searching for your son several times, Beth."

Now I was sitting and he was the one pacing around. I

looked at him in disbelief that he would ever dream of doing such a thing. I was already too stunned by the impact of receiving Mike's letter for Chuck's words to sink in. To hear that he had been thinking along those lines was deeply moving. He looked very happy. By the time the phone rang later on, I was beside myself with anticipation. I picked up the phone and practically whispered, "Hello."

"Hello, is this Beth?" the voice said hesitantly.

What a nice voice, I thought, catching my breath.

"Yes, are you Mike?" My heart was in my throat.

He said, "Yes, I'm Mike."

I don't believe this, I thought, *I'm sitting here talking and hearing the voice of my* . . . —I could not even think the word.

When I heard his big sigh, I realized that he was as nervous as I was. His voice sounded familiar, soothing and comfortable. At first, I was worried I wouldn't know what to say to this perfect stranger who claimed to be a part of me, but somehow the time flew by. We talked for over an hour. Wondering what he looked like, I asked, "What color is your hair?" amazed that a mother would need to ask her child such a question.

He replied with a laugh, "What hair?"

"Oh, that's right. Of course! My father was bald," I told him. "I'm sorry."

"Well," he sighed, "that's why I've been searching for so long. I needed to know that." If a voice could smile, his did, as he continued, "Because I've lost most of mine and I wanted to know what else to expect."

Knowing immediately that we both had the same sense of humor, I smiled and said, "I'm glad I could be of help." Already the feeling was warm and friendly.

Mike said, with another chuckle that sounded familiar, "You know, I always thought I might be Italian, with my black hair and olive complexion, but after reading the file I received from Philip Adams, I see that I'm Irish, English, Dutch, Scotch, German and American Indian. What a shock!

12

All these years, my daughters and I thought that we could be Italian."

As Mike was telling me this, I immediately recognized the words as mine. That is how I had always described my mixed nationalities. I said, "Those are my words as my mother taught me to always go down the list. It's quite a mixture, isn't it?"

Not knowing—not remembering—I had to ask, "Who is Philip Adams?"

"He is the attorney you went to for the adoption."

"Philip Adams," I repeated, embarrassed. "I'm sorry. I don't remember his name." Feeling terrible, I said, "I was at a home for unwed mothers." Shocked that I would talk about this with Chuck listening, I continued, with a sigh, "I was given a false name."

"Justine?" Mike asked before I could tell him.

"How on earth do you know that?"

"It's written on the notes I received from Philip Adams," he answered. "It says, 'Justine from St. Elizabeth's' so I assumed it was a false name."

Because he knew so much about me, it felt unreal to be talking about my past with a stranger over the phone. My deep shameful secret was being exposed, and all I could remember was my false name. Still, he sounded delighted to be talking about this with me, as if it had happened yesterday. He was talking very fast, as if he couldn't believe he actually had found me.

"You have a lot of brothers and sisters," he told me, then he read their names. Everything he was reading to me was like hearing my own voice, hearing my own words to describe my family. The feeling was completely unreal. He sounded happy to be talking to me and amazed to discover so much about himself. Imagine thinking yourself to be one nationality for so many years and then discovering that you are such a mixture.

I asked him what he thought when he heard my voice on

his answering machine, remembering how I had rambled on and on. He told me that he had been on his way up the stairs from the garage with a big bag of groceries in each arm. His wife, Linda, upon entering the kitchen always pushed the button on the answering machine so they could both hear their messages.

Mike said he heard my voice while going up the stairs and as he entered the kitchen, heard me say, "You have found the right person." He said his knees buckled and both bags of groceries slipped out of his arms.

He was stunned that I had received the letter so soon. He immediately called his two daughters, and they were all very happy and excited. He told me he had been searching for me for the past five years. Hearing the excitement in his voice, I could tell that his search had been a long emotional process. I was completely thrilled to know that he had been anxious to find me.

We made a date for the following Sunday for him, his wife and one of his daughters to visit our home. Telling him he had two sisters, two nieces and a nephew was weird, but he was thrilled to learn he had a new, extended family for himself and his daughters.

I couldn't believe the wonderful feeling that came over me when we talked about his daughters, my granddaughters. Mike told me that Seana, his younger daughter, was getting married on Saturday at Lake Tahoe. I had a granddaughter I hadn't known existed a few hours ago, and she was getting married! All this new information was coming too fast.

Although I hesitated to do it, because our conversation was so happy, I knew that I had to tell Mike that one of his sisters had died eight years earlier of brain cancer. I found it difficult to tell him this terrible news. When he told me he was genuinely sorry to hear that, I believed him.

Suddenly he said, "Wait a minute. No way am I going to wait until Sunday to meet you! Have you had dinner yet?"

Looking at my cold dinner sitting in front of me, untouched, and Chuck's empty plate, I lied and said, "No, we haven't." I was getting really excited about the prospect of meeting him.

"Well, why don't we meet in Sacramento?" he asked. "It's an hour from our house and an hour from your house."

I almost shouted, "Great!" and felt unbelievably elated.

I handed the phone to Chuck to work out the details. We would meet in the parking lot of the *El Torito* restaurant at nine o'clock.

Imagine, meeting the son I had never seen, in the parking lot of a restaurant. It was too much! As I ran upstairs to change, I tried to find the words to describe the feeling I was experiencing. I stood in front of a mirror and was shocked to see a gray-haired lady staring at me, because I suddenly felt twenty years old again.

Why? What was happening? *Look at me*, I thought. *I look terrible.* But there was no time to try to look any better. "Well, I am who I am," I said to myself. "Besides, he's forty-five years old. He's not a baby, he's a man."

I didn't believe this. How many unreal events could happen to me in one lifetime? But, if this were true—oh, if only Susan were alive to be here, she would be very happy.

Mike said he had searched for five years. So many things were going through my mind as I was trying to decide what to wear. I felt strange. I had buried all my memories and feelings about the events surrounding the birth of that young man, how it had happened and why I had let him go.

I had been so young.

I really had only two children, Susan and Linda, period. I had never mentioned my first child to anyone except my family. I had thought of him many times, wondering, hoping he hadn't been killed in Vietnam. There had been nothing I could do but hope he was well and happy. To discover that he had been searching for me for five years was an incredible thrill.

What a beautiful gift, for me, his mother, the young

woman who had walked away, alone, from the home in San Francisco for unwed mothers—a sad young woman with her head held high, sure she was doing the right thing. Then Chuck called from downstairs, bringing me back to this planet.

"Are you ready, Beth? Let's get going."

I was in such a trance that I jumped. No time to change. I wondered what my son would think to see a sixty-five-year-old mother in jeans and T-shirt. No! I quickly changed my T-shirt for a colorful rayon blouse. One more look and I decided, not too bad for a new mother. I ran downstairs, jumped into the car and sat next to Chuck.

"Well, Beth, here we go," he said as we backed out of the garage. "Are you ready for this? I'm happy for you, and for me too. Don't worry, everything will turn out fine."

I looked at him with gratitude. As we drove off, I remembered the events of so many years ago. What it had been like to be an unwed pregnant woman in 1947. How society would brand the mother and child, but it would be the child who would suffer the most.

When I had made the agonizing decision for adoption, I had known it was right. Afterwards, I had followed the rules like a good little girl and had buried all my emotions and feelings when I went into an emotional closet. Suddenly, I realized the door of that closet had been opened! I could feel the fresh air hitting my face and my soul. An overwhelming sense of relief came over me.

I cried to myself, "He's alive, he's alive, my baby boy is alive!" A miracle had happened and I was going to see him at last.

With Chuck sitting beside me, I told him, "Thanks for being here for me."

3

RACING TO MEET A STRANGER

Racing along Highway 99, I can't help thinking, *Please, God, get me there safely. I can't die now.* My head is exploding with all these conflicting thoughts. What will he think of me, the woman who gave him up? That couldn't be what I had done. I must have had a good reason at the time, but now it was hard to understand, hard to explain.

I know it takes at least an hour to drive to Sacramento, and I'm thinking an hour will seem like forever. But on the other hand, I need this time to comprehend, or try to comprehend, just what is happening. I'm very anxious to meet this person who claims he is my son. I still can't believe this is happening.

I tell myself, "Beth, you are sitting in this car, on your way to meet a person you gave birth to forty-five years ago. You don't even know your own child, you gave him away, how awful, and now he wants to meet you."

Incredible! Things are happening so fast that I can't keep up with myself. I wonder what he looks like. Is he really who he says he is? Is this all a joke? For the second time in my life, the unthinkable has happened. The first was Susan; she had died, and who would ever imagine that their child will die?

Looking through the window, up to the sky full of bright stars, I think about Susan, how happy she would be to know I was on my way to meet her brother. How strange that sounds, Susan and Linda's brother! Now, the little boy I gave birth to and have never seen is on his way to meet me.

When I gave him up for adoption and walked away from St. Elizabeth's, I followed all the advice given to me. Over and over again I had been told, "Get on with your life, Beth. You did the right thing. Don't think about it."

I remember that.

It was all buried so deep that I'm feeling strange and un-real. Being confused, I'm having a hard time understanding. I cannot stop thinking about it. The shock since receiving the letter today and talking to Mike makes me feel I'm losing my breath. Every once in a while I need to take a deep breath, and Chuck notices.

"Are you okay?" he asks.

"Yes, but I can't believe this is happening."

"Don't worry, Beth. It's great and everything will be fine."

When Mike told me that he had searched for five years, I asked him why had he ever wanted to find me. After all, I gave him away. All of it is very vague, but I do remember how hard it had been to be so near to him for two weeks at St. Elizabeth's and yet not see him, and I remember how I cried all the time and was very depressed.

Suddenly, I realize that Chuck is as anxious as I am to reach Sacramento. I notice the speed we're traveling. In si-lence, I pray that we find the parking lot and that we're both in one piece when we get there. I remember Philip Adams, the attorney who helped me. He must be in his eighties now, and he actually still had my file.

Mike had mentioned having a picture of me holding him, but I knew that couldn't be. He was so excited telling me about it during our phone conversation that I hated to tell him it couldn't have been me or him, because I had never seen him. He had said the picture was definitely me, because there was such a strong resemblance to one of his daughters. When he told me that, I couldn't grasp the thought: having a granddaughter who looks like me, from out of nowhere.

Fortunately, Chuck knows where he is going as we drive the streets of Sacramento looking for the parking lot of the *El Torito* restaurant. I'm glad it's dark. I think, maybe I'll look better. Using the cellular phone, Chuck calls Mike and we find that we are at least fifteen minutes ahead of them. Good, we'll arrive before them, and I might have a chance to calm down. I'm afraid to let myself believe this. How could I be so lucky?

As we find the right parking lot, I'm relieved to see that there are very few cars. Sitting here in the dark car, looking around, I realize that I will never forget this place. The pine trees and the tall flowering jasmine form a secluded corner.

The setting is surprisingly pleasant for a parking lot. Maybe we will have some privacy. A welcome breeze cools the very warm night and with the swaying pine trees and the fragrance of jasmine, I think that the only thing missing is music. When I hear a soft, haunting, sentimental tune coming from my heart, I'm not surprised.

Chuck interrupts my trance, saying excitedly, "Here they are, that's their white pickup." He is beaming. He is going to meet my son, and his stepson, something he never thought he would do. As Mike's white pickup turns into a space almost next to ours, I can see his profile. The make-believe feeling continues.

My mind cries out, *Oh, my God, he's real.*

If this were a movie, trumpets would be blaring. Instead, I hear angels singing. Seeing the outline of his head, I hear my mother whisper in my ear, "He has our family's head, with the knowledge bump." My mother had said that about all the children in our family.

Mike has a beard so I can't see his chin. Chuck jumps

19

out of our car and stands there, and, being tall—six inches over six feet—he can look over the car. Mike's wife, Linda, gets out and walks around to the back of both cars and stands between them. Chuck goes around to join Linda, so they both have a good view. The stage is set.

Mike gets out of his pickup, and I see him, my heart pounding as I look at this beautiful man, my son, for the first time in my life. Spellbound, I want this moment to last forever. My heart opens up as I gaze at this miracle. There he is. My child. I never in my life thought I would see him, but there he is. Thank you, God, for giving me this moment.

I recognize the body and build of my brother, Bill. He has a certain bounce that looks familiar. I cannot comprehend that the baby I had can be this grown man, this stranger. Can it really be him? Suddenly reality breaks in and I realize I am still sitting in the car. I know I can't sit here any longer. I have to get out.

Going out quickly, I just stand there.

Frozen.

I notice the fragrance of the jasmine floating in the pleasant evening air, and the haunting make-believe music starting again. I feel I'm in a fairy tale. We look at each other for a moment, and as we start to walk toward each other, it feels like a slow-motion movie. I see that he is quite tall, probably six feet—several inches taller than me. I feel relieved, for some reason, that Mike is tall and good sized.

I can't take my eyes off him; forty-five years melt away in one magical moment. In a whispering, disbelieving voice, I ask, "Are you really you?" With his head tilted to one side and smiling, I can feel his searching gaze as he looks at me for the first time. As we draw closer and I see his face and expression, my mind and body feel a joy I have never known before.

I see a softness in him and hear him say, "Yes. Hi, Mom," as if he had been waiting a long time for this moment. He sighs; his search is over.

As he looks at me, I wonder what he thinks. I hope he isn't disappointed, a gray-haired sixty-five-year-old woman, a stranger, wearing jeans and a loud blouse. We hug briefly, both of us somewhat embarrassed. Reaching up, I put my hand on the back of his head and say, "You have the knowledge bump."

I was surprised by my gesture, but I knew he wouldn't mind. Putting his hand on the back of his head and not knowing what I am talking about, he repeats, "Knowledge bump?"

Suddenly, he steps back, with his arms spread out as he walks around me, circling me, as though his years of curiosity and questions have been answered, and he exclaims, "You are beautiful!" Not knowing what to make of this, I can't speak. I'm just standing here feeling like a movie star and feeling embarrassed, both at the same time, but thrilled by someone who is so happy to see me.

Later on Mike informs me that it was Philip Adams, looking at my picture from years ago while talking to Mike on the phone, who told him, "She's a looker."

Chuck and Linda stand there watching us, with big smiles on their faces. Chuck asks us to stand together for a picture, so we take our first picture together. Mike with a big smile, with an "I did it!" look all over his face. And me, I look totally stunned and dazed.

Mike introduces me to Linda, and I do the same with Chuck. Awkwardly the four of us start to walk toward the restaurant. I don't know how to behave in this situation, I suddenly realize. Walking next to Linda, I notice how I tower over her, as she is about five feet four and small-framed with a nice figure.

Her hair is dark brown and short, and with her big brown eyes, she is very attractive. At five feet seven, I was the tallest in my family. My brothers and sisters were all rather short. Suddenly I feel very self-conscious walking in front of

21

Mike and Chuck. Why did I wear jeans? Why didn't I dress up?

Linda mentions how excited and happy she is for Mike. I can tell from her voice that searching for me has been one of the most important things in his life. Being in such a fog and deeply moved by what she is saying, I can't respond. My words would sound inadequate. I have the feeling of stepping out of my body and watching myself in a movie.

I had the same feeling when Susan died. The impact of what I feel happening to me at this moment is that immense and powerful.

4

THE FILE WITH MY PAST

As we enter the restaurant, I'm blasted by the cold air and suddenly I'm chilled. Linda thoughtfully puts her sweater around my shoulders. I notice the pleasing atmosphere of the bright and lively restaurant as we find our way to a large booth. Still dazed, I am thrilled when Mike makes a point of sitting next to me. Can this be happening? He's my son, and he wants to sit next to me.

Going through the motions of looking at the menu, I can't even read it. My dinner is still on our table at home, untouched. I order, knowing I won't be able to eat a thing, but Chuck is ready to enjoy his second dinner. Mike is so excited that Linda notices, and with concern says, "Slow down, Mike. Take it easy."

He's talking a mile a minute, losing his breath, while I'm sitting here watching him in utter awe. All I want to do is stare at him, he is so beautiful. Everything feels like a dream, and I'm just watching.

The dream world ends as Mike starts pulling papers out of his file. Handing me a picture of myself holding an infant, I realize I can't remember anything about it and feel extremely embarrassed. Holding the picture in my hand, I say, "That's me, but I don't know who this child is. I know it's not you, because I have never seen you."

I ask myself, *Did I see him and not remember?* No.

"I recognize the photo and the clothes I'm wearing," I tell him, "and I'm standing in front of the Housing Project where we lived when you were born. It's dated February 1948, three months after you were born."

How can I be sitting here, saying those words, "You were born" to him? You. He is the "You." Talking to the child who . . . but all that happened in a different world.

Now Mike is showing me a letter I had written, my handwriting. I know it is mine, but I don't remember writing it. Feeling terrible, I ask myself, *How can I not remember these very important letters and pictures?* I had written the letter to Philip Adams on April 1, 1948. I look at my twenty-year-old handwriting and know it is mine but I have no memory of it.

> Dear Mr. Adams:
>
> I want to thank you for everything you've done for me. I feel so much better now that everything is taken care of and that Johnny will have a good home. Thanks to you and Dr. Olson.
>
> By the way, I haven't forgotten the rice you promised.
>
> Thanks again for everything.
>
> Sincerely yours,

Mike is telling me that after reading my letter along with all the other information in the file, he knows I cared about him and understands more of the story. As I read the letter and hear Mike's words, I can't believe that it is me we are talking about. I know it is, but it is just not penetrating.

He asks about my mentioning the attorney's promise of rice. Feeling awkward, I tell him, "I have to say that I have no idea. I simply have no memory of it."

Now Mike produces a copy of my birth certificate, Chuck's and my marriage license, his father's birth certificate—he even has a picture of where my parents lived when I was born. He shows me a picture of a vacant lot, saying he thinks it might be where the Housing Project was. Looking at the picture, I say, "Oh, yes, I remember now. They tore it down several years ago. Thank God."

Another picture.

Gasping, I say, "My God, that's my brother, Jack, with my mother and nephew."

I can't imagine why the attorney had kept it in his file or, for that matter, why he had all of them in the first place. I can't believe someone could find out so much about me.

I say, "Gosh, I'm glad I had nothing to hide." Then I realize that I had the biggest thing in the world to hide. After keeping this secret for so many years, I realize I'm being exposed, but aside from the embarrassment of not remembering I'm amazed I'm not sorry to be exposed. After all, I'm with my son. To have my past presented to me by this fine young man is wonderful.

How good it feels to be sitting here with the only other person in the world involved with all this information in his file. I can feel his excitement as he sits next to me, his mother. Looking at Chuck, I wonder what he thinks about all this. He and Linda appear to be enjoying themselves and are busy talking about Mike and me. They're both obviously happy for us.

Gazing at me with curiosity, Mike asks, "Why did you name me John?"

I remember how that had happened, and it sounds so trivial that I dread telling him.

"Well, I wanted to name you Harold, after my uncle, but they wouldn't let me. They told me I had to name you after a saint, as that was a policy of St. Elizabeth's." I feel my face turning red. "So, I picked a name out of the air: John."

Watching his expression, I don't think he's offended.

25

Good! Because of the way my explanation sounds, I hope he doesn't think that having had him meant nothing to me. I vaguely remember now. It always bothered me, the way I chose his name.

When Mike starts showing me the attorney's handwritten notes about me, my family, my nationality and religion, I recognize what Mike had read to me earlier on the phone. It was just scribbled information. I have a sudden recollection of sitting in the attorney's office, across from his desk, as he asked me the questions that he needed answered. I remember someone being there with me. On the top of the paper the attorney had noted: "Referred by."

Reading the name now, I don't recognize it. But it must have been my roommate from St. Elizabeth's Home who was with me. Everything is there, even a piece of scrap paper from Uncle Harold's company, in my handwriting and Uncle Harold's, with a list of all the expenses, and what I had borrowed from him.

The four of us are amazed that the cost of a plane ticket from Mississippi was $165.00 and the Pullman train ticket was $100.00 for three days. It is like reading about someone else, not me. St. Elizabeth's charges for the delivery, board and care for me and for my baby for six weeks was only $124.35.

We were astounded at the prices, compared with today's. It seems like such a small amount. It brings it all back, how poor I had been, and how long I worked to pay it back. But how did it get in the file? I remembered receiving a phone call at work from my mother in late February 1948, after Mike was born. She told me that my baby was still at St. Elizabeth's and there were outstanding charges for his board and care for three months. My child was still there!

I thought everything had been taken care of. I remember being horrified to think that he was still there, and not knowing what to do. I didn't have any money, and my mother didn't either. My salary from the bank at that time was only $125.00 a month.

I was paying Uncle Harold $40.00 every month and, of course, my mother $40.00 a month for board and room. So to be told that my child was still in the nursery at St. Elizabeth's and that I owed all that money was devastating. I was sick in my heart and afraid that I would be exposed. I had called my friend who had been with me at St. Elizabeth's. We were not supposed to tell each other our real names, but we had.

She'd had her child and the adoption was complete. She lived in San Francisco and she took me to see the attorney, Mr. Adams. He was very nice, made all the arrangements and told me not to worry about the hospital charges or the adoption. Seeing that scrap of paper of Uncle Harold's with the list of expenses I owed, I now remembered that part of the story.

In 1947, what I borrowed from my uncle was a fortune and repaying it was a heavy burden. I don't know how I could have managed without his and Aunt Beth's help. What would I have done without their love and support? Mike pulls more papers from the file, letters to me from Henry, Mike's father, written while I was in Mississippi. I look at Henry's letters, and my face reddens from embarrassment. Thinking of Chuck's feelings, I just glance at them.

I had not known there were letters from Henry until this moment. Where did they come from? Why are they in this file? I remember that Aunt Beth and Uncle Harold had tried very hard to help me by pressuring Henry for money. Seeing these letters is like seeing a ghost from my past. I'm not feeling very good about all this.

Mike is still very excited as he tells me the attorney had placed him in his adoptive father's arms on April 1, 1948. I just stare at him. Looking at this grown man with a beard and imagining him as an infant is impossible. But to hear, "Placed in my adoptive father's arms," sounds as though I had been unfeeling. Visualizing that scene, even though I wasn't there at the time, it seems terrible to believe that I had let it happen.

My mind in a haze, I frantically look for a concrete memory. Everything is happening too fast. Did I do all of these things? Yes, I must have. Here is all the evidence. It's me we're talking about.

"Look," I said to Mike as I noticed the date on the letter, "that's the same day I wrote my thank-you letter to the attorney. April 1, 1948."

I can see that Mike is very much interested in everything I say. Shaking his head, he says, "Really? The same day?"

"That's nothing," Linda chimes in, smiling. "The same date you signed the adoption papers, August 6, 1948, is the same date, August 6, 1993, that Mike and I went to San Francisco and received your file from Mr. Adams."

Exactly forty-five years.

All four of us are shaking our heads, thinking of the coincidence. It is like pieces of a puzzle that I started putting together forty-five years ago—a puzzle that had never been finished. Being confronted by all these important papers, the pieces of the puzzle are floating around in my mind. I can't find where they belong in the puzzle. Humiliated by all of this, I can't think of an explanation for my poor memory.

"I'm sorry, I don't remember," is all I can say.

Mike informs me that it's not unusual for mothers like me to not remember. I hope he isn't disappointed in what he has found for a mother, or that he finds me unfeeling because I'm in such shock. I wonder what Chuck is thinking as I glance at him. This is all new information to him. I can see he's very happy for me, and that he feels and understands my shock and sense of exposure.

"I'm happy you found me," I tell Mike. "I never would have searched for you. I have always felt I didn't have the right to search for you. I wondered about you many times. I had a strong feeling you were killed in Vietnam." Looking him in the eyes, I go on. "You were the right age. I remember thinking that all during the war, but I had no way of knowing. I always hoped you were alive and well."

Then I take a deep breath for courage.

"I want you to know, Mike, that I have never felt guilty and have always thought I did the right thing."

Saying that, now I wonder. Am I feeling guilt? I gave this man, when he was a baby, to someone else, and yet here he is looking at me with delight.

"When the attorney gave me your file last Friday," Mike says with a smile, "things happened fast. We went to the Alameda County Court House to check the records and I knew for sure that it was you I had found. From there we drove all over Oakland, taking pictures of houses you had lived in. Looking at property records, we picked up your last address in San Leandro and discovered you had moved to Stockton."

He is excited, telling me this, and so is Linda. They're both talking at the same time. We're all laughing and having a great time.

Then Mike says, "We even found your house in Stockton. That night. We parked across the street. I was tempted and wondered if I should knock on your front door. Then we decided we'd better not."

I realize I've never had anyone so interested in me in my whole life. Their eagerness is so apparent, Mike and Linda's. Astounded by what I have just heard, all I can say is, "You're kidding!"

Smiling, getting a kick out of all this too, Chuck asks, "Did you really? Park across the street?"

"Yes, and Sunday night too, with the motor home, on our way back from the Bay Area."

I am flabbergasted, hearing how they had us under surveillance, twice, and we were totally unaware of it. As they revealed their sleuthing abilities, I could feel their excitement, like a great mystery adventure they were on. I'm on the receiving end of all this and I'm very happy.

29

Laughing, I say, "Boy, you did all that? Receiving the Special Delivery letter today was a humdinger! If you had knocked on our front door the other night, I would have passed out."

We're all laughing. I have this wonderful feeling of elation as I notice Mike and I have the same sense of humor. It's comforting sitting next to him, this man, who was so anxious to find me. I like what I see in him, and can feel how much his finding me means to him. This is all new, and I feel wonderful. Free.

I can't wait to get to know him better. I still can't believe he is my son, but why does he feel so familiar, like my brother Bill? His neck and shoulders are the same as Bill's. I wish I could see Mike without his beard. His father was only twenty-three when I last saw him, so I can't tell if there is a resemblance. Maybe his coloring. Mike has an olive complexion and brown eyes, as Henry did. But his physique and demeanor are like my brother Bill's.

Someone mentions that it's getting late and we all have a long drive home. Already? I hate to leave. I didn't get a chance to say anything about what's going on inside me. I'm too confused anyway. I only know I like sitting next to him and looking at him. He is so beautiful. And he has a great smile.

Walking back to the parking lot, Mike excitedly tells me, "So many times through my life, everywhere I went I fantasized meeting you. At airports, train stations, even waiting in line at the grocery store and banks, I would look at everyone, looking for a resemblance, wondering if you were there. I can't believe I found you and that this is really happening."

He stops.

"Do you know there are twenty-three women across the United States with your name? I searched them all, and you were next to the last, number twenty-two. When I finally got the name of your attorney, it was fast. It only took a few days. I can't believe it. I'm glad I found you."

"Did you say twenty-three women? And you searched them all out?"

My God, I feel like a celebrity. I am touched by his enthusiasm and sincerity. He is so happy. Why isn't he angry for what I did to him?

We plan our reunion for Sunday at our home with our daughter Linda, our granddaughter Guinevere, and Mike's daughter Kim. Because his other daughter, Seana, is getting married on Saturday, she will not be at the family reunion.

As we say goodbye, Mike wraps his arms around me and we hug. I am reminded of my brother again. I feel someone familiar, and a pull that's very deep and haunting, as if I have found the core of peace, of joy, as if I have known him all my life. I have found something that had been there all the time, and I hadn't even known it. My son.

In a quiet voice, I say, "Thank you so much for finding me."

"Thank you for waiting for me to find you," he answers softly.

Driving off, I'm overwhelmed with countless unfamiliar emotions. I hope Mike is not disappointed in me, the way I acted, being confused. But I can't worry about that now, I'm just too happy.

Chuck is saying something.

Deep in thought, I have to ask him to repeat it.

"Well, Beth, you must be happy. He seems like a great guy. I have a son—well, almost a son. Now I'll have another guy to talk to. This is good and I'm happy for you."

It must be after midnight when we pull into the garage. Entering the house, everything feels strange. There is a feeling of tranquillity that I hadn't felt before. I realize my world has changed. The child I gave away is back. Climbing into bed, I am filled with strange, unfamiliar emotions. I start to cry, then I'm happy, then I'm sad. *Please, God, let this all be true.*

Lying in bed, thinking about everything I saw in the file the attorney gave Mike and trying to piece it together, I think of 1947, what it was like all those years ago.

I start to remember all of it.

Everything that happened to me, and just exactly the way it was.

5

REMEMBERING JUSTINE—1947

As the plane made its landing at the San Francisco Airport, I was captivated by the beauty of San Francisco and the Bay. The skyline was breathtaking. The crisp weather of the late October day made the sky a brilliant blue with mounds of white, whipped cream clouds. With the sun shining on it, the water sparkled like the jewel that it was.

I felt relieved to be home, where I belonged.

The pilot had announced during the flight that if we walked to the back of the plane, we would be walking at two hundred miles an hour. I remember thinking that was unbelievable. I wanted to try it, but with the stewardess keeping a close eye on me, I remained in my seat. I remember how excited I was to feel the thrust of the takeoff when the plane left Mississippi. It was my first flight and the most thrilling experience I had ever had.

The year was 1947, and the plane was a twin-engine, propeller-driven DC3. I thought it was immense with its three seats across. I gripped the armrest when we took off. I would have enjoyed the adventure of the flight much more if I hadn't felt the constant attention and hovering of the stewardess.

I was eight months pregnant, and the airline was not happy about my being on their plane. They almost hadn't let me on. So while our arrival in San Francisco was a relief for the stewardess, it held a fear of the unknown for me.

My mother and stepfather were there to meet me. Even though my mother knew I was pregnant, I could see that she was shocked to see how I had changed from her slim young daughter to this huge swollen figure. Three months earlier, when she put me on the train to Mississippi, she had not expected to see me back so soon, or looking so pregnant.

As we left the airport in my stepfather Charlie's car, I tried to hide on the floor of the back seat.

"What are you trying to do, Beth?" my mother asked, astounded. "You'll hurt yourself."

I struggled to find a way to keep the bulk of my pregnancy out of the sight of passing cars.

"Mother," I groaned, "if anyone who knows me sees that I'm pregnant, I'll be ruined forever." As I tried to find a comfortable way to hide, I continued, "I'm still supposed to be out of town, remember?"

My mother turned around and did not say another word. I knew this was hard on her. I had noticed she hadn't hugged me when I arrived, and I wished she could have seen that I needed a hug. I remembered her crying when she put me on the train for Mississippi. Maybe she thought she would not have to worry about me or my condition.

My condition was that of a twenty-year-old, unmarried pregnant woman. My condition, at that time, was shocking and scandalous. So scandalous that I had to quit my job and run away to keep my pregnancy a secret. In 1947, I would have been considered a loose and immoral woman. The baby would have been labeled illegitimate and could have been branded forever.

I tried to be invisible as we arrived at the downtown hotel. It was degrading to feel like a criminal. I knew what people said about women like me, society's outcasts. It was not easy to remember that I was still me, not the immoral woman that people might point a finger at. I was tired of feeling bad about myself, tired of agonizing over the decision that I still had to make.

I recall the hotel was either on Montgomery Street or Geary Street, close to Market. Entering our room, I had been impressed.

"This hotel is nice, Mom. It must cost a lot of money."

She said that Uncle Harold had paid for the room, which explained why it looked expensive. It was bright and sunny. If only I could have been there under different circumstances.

What would I have done without Uncle Harold? I had already borrowed so much from him. The train, the plane, the hotel and the expenses of St. Elizabeth's Hospital for me and the delivery of my baby. He and Aunt Beth had been so good to me. I must let them know how much I appreciated everything and tell them I would pay back every penny, if it took forever.

Arriving at the hotel around dinnertime was a problem. We had to eat, but I remember my fear of going out in public. Mother and Charlie talked me into going with them to Foster's Cafeteria close to our hotel. Because it was impossible to hide the fact that I was eight months pregnant, I was in constant fear of being seen and recognized.

When mother called St. Elizabeth's the next morning, we received what to me was devastating news. They would not accept me without a blood test. The delay would force me to hide for another twenty-four hours.

St. Elizabeth's informed my mother that we would have to go to the Flood Building on Market Street for the blood test. Market Street! The busiest street in San Francisco! I just about died. When Charlie pulled to the curb near the Flood Building and I had to get out of his car, being big and pregnant I was in a panic as I tried to run across the wide sidewalk. Waiting for the elevator was agony.

35

"Beth, stop worrying," mother kept saying. "There are a lot of people in San Francisco and the chance of your being seen by someone you know is almost impossible."

I didn't believe her.

The whole experience added to my shame. While taking my blood test, I felt everyone was looking at me. They knew I was an unwed mother, waiting to go into a "home." We would not know the results of the blood test until the next day. I thought, *God, this is terrible. We can't go back to the hotel. Where will I hide all day?*

Mother decided that Charlie would drop us off in front of a small theater around the corner from the St. Francis Hotel. It's strange, but I still remember the name of the movie, a foreign film called, "Black Narcissus." Later, Charlie would pick us up and take us to another hotel.

Uncle Harold had only paid for one night at the nice hotel. My mother had stayed there with me the first night, but not the second. I still cannot believe my mother took me to that terrible second hotel, over a restaurant. It was a cheap, run-down flophouse on Fillmore Street, not a good area even in 1947, and on Halloween night at that.

I remember that having to spend a night alone in such a sleazy place was horrifying. How could my mother leave me there, knowing I was eight months pregnant? The building was ancient, probably from the early 1900s, the kind of building that has rooms for rent above the stores.

I don't think it was even a hotel; I don't remember a lobby, only stairs from the street. It had a rundown, neglected feel to it. I could imagine what went on in some of the other rooms. Obviously, Charlie had made the arrangements before we arrived. As we walked down the dark, narrow hall, I noticed that everything was dirty and gray and poorly painted. When we got to the room I was to stay in, there was just a wooden door, with a transom and a big keyhole for an old-fashioned skeleton key.

My room was the same dingy gray, and I could see that

the painted wainscoting was dark and dirty. There was an adjoining room with another flimsy door and another big keyhole with the key in it. I wondered who was staying in that room. I think my room shared the bathroom with that other room, because there was another door in the bathroom and another keyhole. I remember being afraid to use the bathroom, feeling that someone could be peeping through the keyhole.

The furniture was old and worn and the bed creaked, so all through the night I was afraid to move. But first, we hadn't had dinner, so my stepfather went to the restaurant under my room and bought me a plate of food. I remember a hot roast beef sandwich and some string beans. I think Charlie had to take the plate and silverware back because I remember him and my mother waiting patiently for me to eat. I wondered what he had told the people in the restaurant about me and my being alone upstairs.

I didn't have anything to read, and I needed to keep my mind occupied, especially when I learned my mother would not be staying. I asked Charlie to buy me a magazine. I can't imagine why, but he bought a horoscope magazine for the whole month of November, as if I didn't know what my month of November would be like at St. Elizabeth's. I remember reading it to see what "adventure" I would have had.

Because it was Halloween, the streets that evening were very noisy with goblins and ghosts, loud shouting voices and police sirens. I was frightened and deeply hurt and angry. I must have cried for hours.

Somehow I made it through the night. With the results of the blood test in hand, we arrived in the early afternoon at the impressive red brick building called St. Elizabeth's Home for Unwed Mothers. I was relieved, beginning to feel safe. Walking slowly through the big double doors, I entered a new world. I knew I was starting on the final stages of my pregnancy and would be able to think more clearly about the decision I still had to make.

37

Mother and I nervously waited in the great hall, not knowing what to expect. Hearing the approach of Mother Superior, we could feel her presence and power even before we saw her. With the resounding rustle of her heavy habit and beads and the thunderous echo of her shoes on the marble floor, mother and I were frozen in awe as Mother Superior rounded the corner.

Seeing her large, round body swathed in her black habit, with the big white starched collar against her round face, I was fear-struck as mother and I followed her into her office. Aunt Beth had already arrived and looked anxious. She must have been surprised to see me so big and pregnant, but she smiled and hugged me and told me she liked my hair short. I thanked her and could not think of anything else to say. Then I asked her to thank Uncle Harold for everything and promised I would pay him back.

Mother Superior sat behind her big desk and, in a sober attitude, informed us of the gravity of the rules and policies of St. Elizabeth's. My work duties would be to set the tables before the meals and clear up after the meals. She thought it was nice for me to arrive on All Saints Day, November 1, a Feast Day, with special privileges and food.

Mother Superior had a stern look on her round face when she assigned me my new name, the name I was to go by at St. Elizabeth's. She warned that I was not to talk about myself with the other mothers-to-be, and that I was not to mention my last name. She frowned, looking directly at me.

"The rules are only to protect you"—she looked down to remember the false name she had assigned me—"Justine, in case you are ever to meet or see one of the other unwed mothers again."

I remember feeling that Mother Superior knew how to make me aware of my condition and the shame of it. I was humiliated to be spoken to like that in front of my mother and Aunt Beth. She did not know anything about me, or my story. She could not care less about me and my baby. It was obvious that Mother Superior was not a warm and compassionate person.

Justine! What an unusual name. I thought it odd to have a false name, and it made me feel false. Then the subject of adoption was mentioned. It was assumed that I had decided to give up my baby. I did not tell Mother Superior, but I still had not made up my mind. I was already distressed by Mother Superior's attitude toward me, and I prayed I would not have to spend much time with her. When she stood, we knew the time was up.

She informed me I would be allowed one visitor for the duration of my stay.

As we said good-by, Aunt Beth told me, "I'll come to visit you in about three weeks, Bethie. It's easier for me, because your mother lives further away, in Oakland. Besides, you will need the clothes that you left at our house before you went to Mississippi. Is that all right with you, Alva?"

Mother said yes, and thanked Aunt Beth for all that she and Uncle Harold had done for me. I tearfully thanked them both for all their help and told them not to worry about me, as I felt safe and settled. They both looked sad, and I felt sorry for them.

As they walked out, the big double doors banged closed, and the sound reverberated through the great hall—and through me. The world was shut out. I could stop pretending. I was left standing with the terrifying Mother Superior. What if all the nuns were like her? I trembled, thinking about it. Mother Superior waited for another nun to take me off her hands and show me around.

To my relief and delight I could see that Sister Mary was much younger, and much smaller. She was actually smiling at me. I tried to return her smile as Sister Mary showed me where I would live for the next six weeks or so. We entered another set of double doors that had an "off limits" look. The living quarters for the mothers-to-be.

The place was a pleasant contrast to the attitude of Mother Superior. It was nice, warm and friendly. Wide hallways. Several dormitory-like rooms with four sections each. I could see that each expectant mother had her own space and could feel private. The curtains, bedspreads and other small touches helped to make each section seem less institutionalized.

As we entered a large room that was furnished with an assortment of comfortable couches and chairs, I could see tables for puzzles and games, and bookshelves that were full. I was impressed with the feeling it had of a nice home. The tall windows even had pretty drapes and curtains. It was certainly furnished better than my mother's home. Someone had obviously tried to make this room feel like home, though it was probably not Mother Superior.

I was struck by the realization that all these women were pregnant, just like me. I had forgotten where I was for a moment. Now I felt I could relax for the first time in months. We were all pregnant, we were all unwed, and I did not have to feel ashamed around these women. I felt much better. All the women were in various stages of pregnancy and were different shapes and sizes. They smiled at me, but no one volunteered her name. I guessed their ages to be from sixteen to thirty.

Everyone looked at me with envy. It was obvious from my size that I did not have long to go. Some of these women still had four or five months to wait. No wonder they envied me. As I gazed around this large, pleasant room and looked more closely at these women, I thought we were lucky to be here.

6

LEARNING TO BE JUSTINE

Sister Mary and I continued our tour. When we finally arrived at the room assigned to me, I was surprised to find that it was a private room, with twin beds, two chairs and a vanity dresser. The beds were high, like hospital beds.

My bed was against the back wall by a tall, narrow window that looked out at the roof of the floor below. I didn't mind because at night I could look at the sky and see the stars. I noticed that I had my own bathroom, because adjoining my room was the janitor's storage room, with a toilet and shower.

I did not share this room with anyone, and at the time I wondered why. Now I think it was because I only had a month to go before I was due. Sister Mary stayed with me as I unpacked the few things I had brought. She informed me that I could borrow some smocks and maternity skirts. I was happy to hear that, as the skirt I had on was far too tight for me now. I only had two smocks, and I was really sick of looking at them.

Sister Mary asked, "Are you planning to give up your child for adoption, Justine?"

I hesitated before answering.

"Yes, I think so."

Sister Mary smiled and said, "It's the right thing to do, Justine. You must think of the child. When is your due date?" The term "due date" was new to me.

I answered, "Well, the doctor said I should have the baby around the first of December. So I guess I won't be here too long."

Sister Mary smiled again and nodded as she looked at the size of me.

"You look as if you only have a month to go," she said. "I'm sure you know that you will stay for two weeks after the baby is born. If your child is adopted, you must wait to see that the child doesn't have any problems."

"Yes," I answered. "Mother Superior told me that if there was anything wrong with the baby, it would be a problem. I guess people only want perfect babies."

It seemed as if we were talking about someone else, not me. Sister Mary pulled her pocket watch out of her habit to check the time.

"Don't worry about your baby having problems, Justine. You look healthy to me."

This was all getting very real. I suddenly felt sad. I was going to have a baby, and that baby would have to be perfect, or no one would want it. How terrible. I felt like screaming.

Of course, I didn't scream.

I smiled and said, "Thank you."

Sister Mary said we should see the chapel downstairs on our way to the dining rooms. She mentioned that we would be having a feast because of All Saints Day. The chapel was beautiful, peaceful and quiet. Sister Mary asked if I attended church. I smiled, shrugged and said, "Not very much."

With a knowing look she said, "Father Brown hears confessions on Thursdays and Fridays if you care to go to Holy Communion. If you have not been to confession yet, you will feel better when you do, and you can receive forgiveness for your sins. Think about it, Justine."

I said, "You're right, Sister Mary," as I hung my head. I felt terrible about myself. Again, I wanted to scream. *God, what had I done?*

"You're right," I repeated. "I should go to confession, and I will."

I was happy to leave the chapel when we headed for the dining rooms. Smelling the delicious food, I was reminded that I hadn't eaten since breakfast. There were two dining rooms, both with four or five round tables for six. The tables were set very nicely with tablecloths and attractive dishes and silverware that shined. Each table had flowers. I learned later that the flowers were in celebration of the Holy Day.

Sister Mary showed me to my seat and introduced me to the other young unwed mothers. Some names come back to me: Nancy, who was only four months pregnant, Mary, Sara, Michele and one other—and now me, Justine. At another table close by there was an expectant mother whose false name was my real name, Beth. I thought that I would have to be careful. If I heard her being called, I might answer, then everyone would know my name.

Nancy asked when my due date was. There was that term again. It seemed to be popular at St. Elizabeth's.

"The doctor said I should deliver around the first of December," I answered.

They told me how lucky I was to only have a month left. Due dates—that was all they talked about. Much of it was about the other expectant mothers who didn't know when their due dates were. They giggled when they talked about one of the mothers who had already delivered. They said she was so far off the due date that it was obvious she had the dates all wrong. That proved that the mother was loose and immoral.

I finally realized what they were talking about. Even in this home for unwed mothers, you could be made to feel cheap. We all felt that if we delivered on time, it would prove that we were not really bad, because our mistake had only happened once or twice. I prayed that I delivered on time. I knew that eventually I would tell them my story, about how I had come to be sitting at the same table with them, in the same condition.

The food was good and was served family-style. I remember the luxurious pleasure of being able to have seconds. We all enjoyed the fact that we could eat as much as we wanted. Once again, I was impressed, as I had been about the huge activity room where the women spent so much time.

Someone wanted us to have enough good food in pleasant surroundings, so we would feel at home. I thought that was very nice. Maybe Mother Superior wasn't so bad after all. After dinner, I started my duty of clearing the tables. I met the nuns who were responsible for all the good meals we had. The sisters were nice to me as I learned how to set the tables for the next day's morning meal. It was not a hard task, and it offered the opportunity for extra food.

I was very tired when I went to my room that first evening. It had been a long, emotional day and I had a lot to think about. I felt sad as I climbed into bed in this strange new room, but I felt safe as I remembered the fear I had felt for me and my baby the night before in that horrifying hotel room.

I put my hands on my stomach and said, "My baby." How could my mother have let me stay in that awful place alone? How could I keep my baby and take it home to my mother's house? How could I do that?

What could I do?

7

BEING JUSTINE

A wave of sadness swept over me as I tried to find a comfortable way to sleep on my side. At least I could see
the stars. I started crying. Yes, I had a lot to think
about. How had this happened to me? How could I have been
such a fool? I thought he loved me. I thought we were going
to be married. Why? What would I do?

I needed to stop feeling sorry for myself and decide.
They told me the child would be better off adopted, with a
mother and father, good people with a home and money. Ed-
ucated people, with the ability to provide a good life for the
child. Not like us: poor, living in the Housing Project, with
drinking and fighting.

Illegitimate. *My God, my baby would be illegitimate.* It
was not fair. It was not the baby's fault; it was my fault. I was
sorry when I thought of my behavior, and embarrassed for
Aunt Beth and Uncle Harold, for everyone to know what I
had done.

I remembered, after telling Aunt Beth I was pregnant,
that facing Uncle Harold had been one of the hardest things
I had ever had to do. Uncle Harold always stood over the sink

and looked out the window as he drank his morning coffee. As I walked into the kitchen, I saw the tears in his eyes.

I told him how sorry I was to have this happen while living in his home. He and Aunt Beth had always been good to me. As I stood there next to him, looking out the window, he put his arm around me and told me not to worry; he would help me in every way he could. I cried with relief when he told me that. He let me know I could depend on his and Aunt Beth's support and that they still loved me.

It seemed like so many months ago, but I remembered sitting on the edge of Aunt Beth's bed later that same day and feeling numb. I sat there, nodding my head in agreement with everything she said. I was going to my brother's house in Mississippi, telling everyone my sister-in-law, Sue, was ill and needed my help.

"Bethie," my aunt told me, "before you go to Mississippi, you must know that if you keep that baby, it will ruin both of your lives. You might never meet a man who will want to marry you with an illegitimate child."

I listened, my heart heavy with the shock that I was pregnant, feeling bitterly ashamed.

"If you keep the baby," Aunt Beth continued in a sad voice, "you will have to take it to your mother's house, and then what will happen?" With a big sigh, she started to cry. "Give the child up for adoption, Bethie. It is the right thing to do for the child, and better for you too."

I could not say a word because I knew Aunt Beth was right, but it sounded cold and final. I remember thinking, *I guess I will have to do what she says*.

"Give the baby up, Bethie. Then forget it, put it all behind you and get on with your life."

She became very intense and started smiling at the same time, as if she had seen some glimmer of hope.

"Go back to the bank. You have a good start there already, you're a good worker and you look good. You can start all over. No more mistakes. Someday Prince Charming will come along and give you an engagement ring. So, for the child's sake and yours, Bethie, have the baby adopted."

Fortunately, Aunt Beth and Uncle Harold's daughter was at school that day. I was very close to my cousin, Harilyn, who was soon to be twelve. It had been difficult dealing with my situation and trying to keep it from her. She was far too young to know, but I could tell that she saw something was going on.

Because I was like a big sister to her and she looked up to me, I was ashamed for her to know. I left Aunt Beth's home on Harilyn's birthday on my way to Mississippi. I remember the sadness on her face as she waved good-bye thinking I wouldn't be gone long.

That had been more than three months ago. I knew my aunt had given me good advice, but that advice had been given before I could feel the baby inside me, before I became attached to it and talked to it—before I realized this child was such a part of me. I started crying again. I was angry, and it all seemed unfair.

All my life I had been working toward my goals. This was not my goal, to be labeled an unwed mother. No. My goals, I thought, my goals had started when I was a little girl.

I had been about three years old the first time my mother sent me to San Francisco to keep me away from my father. He did not like me. I heard that all my life, but no one ever told me why. My mother told me that my father wanted her to spank me, even at nine months old.

By the time I was three, I guess the fear was too much. My oldest brother, Bill, was eleven years older than me and when I was three he hit my father with a baseball bat and knocked him out. My father was hitting my mother because of me. My father must have been drunk. He was an alcoholic, and he was not a nice man.

The day we left my father, I was seven years old. I pulled my red wagon along the street to our new house, and my father didn't know we were leaving him. I remembered not being sorry to go. My mother had married again two years later. My stepfather was a kind man, but he gambled. We never had enough money or food and we were always moving, at least once a year, because we couldn't pay the rent.

So from age three I started going back and forth between Aunt Beth and Uncle Harold's house and my mother's home in Oakland. I started my rags-to-riches-to-rags childhood. And I started setting my goals for life.

In San Francisco with my aunt and uncle, I was a little princess, the only child around all adults. I had my own room, with warm milk and cookies before being tucked into bed each night. I had a Shirley Temple doll, and a navy blue princess-style coat with a Peter Pan collar. The collar and the lining were a bright print of Snow White and the Seven Dwarfs. I loved that coat and was constantly holding it open so everyone could see the lining. I was loved.

They wanted to adopt me, but my mother said no. From ages three to fifteen I went back and forth between my two homes. Whenever I went back to my mother's, it was always to a new house and a new school. Never enough food or money. Always poor, always fighting, always booze, and we ended up living in a Housing Project with other people like us.

At eighteen, I had started working at the Federal Reserve Bank, in a good position. I had moved to San Francisco to live with Aunt Beth and Uncle Harold because it would be easier than commuting. My mother was upset.

The war had just ended, the war-related jobs were over and if I was not living there with my mother, I would not be paying my room and board. Every payday I sent her money anyway. I knew I could, and would, do better with my life. I had wanted to have a home and a life like my aunt and uncle. I had gotten a good start by working at the bank.

As I lay in my strange new room at St. Elizabeth's, I sobbed as I thought about what I had done to my life, especially while living with Aunt Beth and Uncle Harold. If only I had not fallen for Henry's lies. I thought he loved me. He had acted as if he did. I had been working at the bank for six months before Henry started there. I was well thought of and was considered a good employee. I was efficient and accurate and balanced my work.

Those of us with more experience would help the newcomers balance their work. The whole Transit Department had to balance before we could leave for the day. There had been lots of young people; many were servicemen returning home after World War II. Sometimes we would work late and all of us would go out to dinner afterwards. It was fun being young and single in San Francisco in 1946.

One day, as I was standing at my work station by my adding machine, four tall, impressive people walked through our department—two men and two women. All four of them looked like models, and everyone stopped and stared as they went by. One of the men was Henry.

After a couple of weeks, Henry started working at the station behind mine. He would say flattering things about me to another woman, letting her know he was interested in me, knowing she would tell me. When I finished my work, he would ask me to help him.

Whenever we had to work late, Henry and I always worked together. He pursued me and I was flattered. I thought he was a very sophisticated twenty-five-year-old. He was only twenty-two, but I was a naive nineteen-year-old and believed everything he said. We went out several times and became engaged on New Year's Eve. About four months later he broke our engagement by leaving a note in my time card slot, stating he was not ready to get married.

I was stunned and brokenhearted.

Everyone at work knew we had been engaged and most knew he had broken our engagement, so when a month later he announced that he was getting married in July, everyone was shocked. Trying to understand, I realized that he must already have been living with the other woman while engaged to me.

Henry got married in July, so continuing to work at the bank with him every day was humiliating. When I finally admitted to myself that I must be pregnant, I went to see a doctor. My heart sank when he told me I was more than four months pregnant. What was I going to do?

When I told Henry about it just two weeks after he got married, he said, "What do you want me to do, divorce my wife and marry you?"

Mortified, I couldn't believe his insulting remark. Showing my disgust, I looked him in the eye and said, "I would not marry you, Henry, if you were the last man on earth." How could I have ever believed him? Later, I heard rumors that his new wife was also pregnant. He was a cad, and I was ashamed of the whole affair.

While lying there in my bed, looking at the stars, I must have been awake for hours. I realized that I had to pull myself together, and how important it was for me to make the right decision. I felt very sad and alone.

Suddenly I was startled by a very strong kick. I smiled and remembered that I was not alone at all. My baby was still with me.

We finally went to sleep.

8

LIVING THE LIE

I spent the next few days adjusting to the routine at St. Elizabeth's. I didn't feel like spending time in the activity room, because the other expectant mothers were knitting booties and other baby things. That bothered me. I didn't feel like talking to anyone either, so I stayed in my room. I was very depressed.

For the first time since I had discovered I was pregnant, I was able to be quiet and alone and not be around anyone I knew. It was a relief not to be living a lie. I had started lying as soon as I found out I was pregnant. I had lied when I left the bank, saying my sister-in-law in Mississippi was gravely ill, and I was the only family member who was single and able to go take care of her.

Between Aunt Beth and Uncle Harold we had invented this same story to tell all the relatives. My oldest brother Bill was an Army officer stationed in Mississippi, and he and his wife Sue had agreed to take me in. Uncle Harold arranged for me to travel first-class on a Pullman. The train trip took three days and nights from Oakland to Mississippi. Wearing my dime-store wedding ring and Aunt Beth's expensive lavender suit with a print blouse, I looked very much the married woman.

In the Pullman car, the seats faced each other and were upholstered with a dark wine-colored mohair or velvet. The drapes were the same wine color, lined for darkness while sleeping, I guessed. The interior trim was a dark wood that looked like mahogany. It was elegant, first-class, just as I had seen in the movies.

A woman and her small child sat across from me. I didn't look pregnant yet, and I was glad she wouldn't notice. She started talking and asking me questions. Seeing my wedding band, she assumed I was married, so I started telling my lies.

I was on my way to Mississippi, I began, to meet my husband who was returning home from overseas. I tried not to say too much because I didn't know what I was talking about. I wondered if she was going to ask questions about myself for three days, so I became aloof and buried my nose in my book. The woman was merely being polite, but I was so sick at heart that I didn't want to talk to anyone, let alone make up lies.

I was fascinated watching the steward set up the berths. Like a jigsaw puzzle, every piece fit perfectly together to make comfortable beds. Long drapes hung from the ceiling to the floor for complete privacy.

When my bed was made up, I went to the ladies' room and changed into my aunt's very proper satin pajamas and robe. The ladies' room was not very private for changing clothes and when I removed my skirt and jacket, anyone could see that I was pregnant. I felt that everyone knew my condition just by looking, as if I were wearing a sign, and I wondered if I would ever feel normal again. I remember being embarrassed to walk down the aisle in my bathrobe.

Uncle Harold had even arranged for me to have the lower berth and once I was in bed and alone, I could shut out the world. I hadn't wanted to cry because someone might hear me. I looked out at the sky and bright stars and wondered again how this could be happening to me.

As I gazed at the stars, I remembered Aunt Beth, only three weeks ago, suggesting we shop for new clothes for me. My skirts had been getting tight, but I had thought I was just gaining weight. Now I realized that she had known I was pregnant before I had told her. I understood why Aunt Beth had looked at me the way she had. She had wanted me to tell her.

Henry had told me that due to a war injury he was sterile and we had a long discussion about not being able to have children. What a fool I had been. Now I knew why he had lied, and it made me feel more embarrassed to know I had been so stupid.

I kept telling myself I couldn't be pregnant, that I was just late—as I have been all my life. But I knew. I just couldn't face it. I couldn't believe it had happened to me. But it had. If Aunt Beth could see it, did everyone at the bank see it too? They must have noticed. Maybe that's why Henry had left the bank so soon after he got married.

I had been quiet and sad all the time. My closest friend Nora noticed and finally asked me what was wrong. I told her and she took me to her doctor. Sitting in the doctor's office, I had been ashamed to tell him that I thought I might be pregnant. My first words to him were that I had been engaged. I hadn't wanted him to think that I was the type of girl who was loose.

It was my first experience having a doctor examine me, and he confirmed my suspicions. My heart dropped when he had told me I was about four and a half months pregnant.

Full of remorse and disgusted with myself as I lay in my berth on the speeding train, I buried my face in my pillow and sobbed. Finally, with the continuous sounds of the rocking train and an occasional haunting whistle I drifted off to sleep.

Waking up the next morning and looking out the window, I wished I could have stayed in the privacy of the berth all day. But the steward went through the same routine with the berths, putting all the pieces together again, like magic. I went to the dining car and sat alone. Although I looked at the menu and saw what the other passengers were eating, I could only afford coffee and toast.

Looking out the window at the passing landscape, the desert of Arizona was all new to me; there were hundreds of cactus plants and nothing else. It was fascinating to see such a big expanse of nothing but desert. Later that day as we went through New Mexico, I saw many Indians. The train stopped so the passengers could purchase items from the crafts displayed, but I was afraid to take a chance, fearful the train would take off without me.

Before leaving San Francisco, I had given myself a ridiculous married name and every time the steward talked to me he would call me by that name. Sometimes I would forget the name and not realize he was talking to me. I wasn't good at this game of lying and traveling under a false identity. No one cared but me, but the fear of exposure was overwhelming. I had to keep my secret, even on the train.

My seat partner and her child had moved to another empty place on the train. I guessed she might have thought I was rude, but I couldn't take a chance on being too friendly and talkative. I might have said the wrong thing and been exposed.

The desert of New Mexico and Texas became boring after a while. When we reached the eastern side of Texas, everything changed. For the first time in my life, I saw shanties—rows of shanties along the railroad tracks. Poor black people lived there. I could see right through their houses. Just boards of wood, with spaces between.

No windows or doors. Barefoot little kids playing in the dirt. I was appalled at the poverty. Soon, that was all I saw. Dirt roads and tumbledown shacks. An occasional old beat-up car. Many children with adults sat listlessly on the porches of their shanties. They looked so hopeless. I had thought I was poor, but I had never seen anything like this in my life. I had heard how black people were treated in the South, but it was horrible to see and I felt bad for them.

California had not been like this at all. It was a sight I would never forget. After seeing the way the blacks were treated, I wondered what it would be like in Mississippi, which is really in the deep South.

Bill and Sue met me at the train station when I arrived. The first thing I noticed about Jackson, Mississippi was the weather. It was always damp and sticky from the terrible heat and humidity. As soon as I took a shower and dried myself, I was wet again. Being pregnant and not used to this climate, all I wanted to do was sit. I knew I should have been taking walks for exercise, but the heat devastated me.

One day, I walked to the nearest grocery store. After about three blocks of nice houses and paved streets and sidewalks, everything suddenly changed. The houses were dilapidated and ramshackle. No sidewalks or paved streets, just dirt. There was a dusty grit on everything, even on the trees and bushes. It was the black section.

I walked into the grocery store and the people were nice, but they stared at me with curiosity. The store didn't have much of a selection and the meat and produce looked bad. Later, telling my brother where I had gone, he warned me never to do that again. He explained that in the South a white woman never goes into a black neighborhood.

On another occasion I took the bus downtown to meet my sister-in-law. This was my first experience seeing black people forced to sit at the back of the bus. All the seats were taken in the back, but many blacks were standing even though there were empty seats in the front.

Another time, while walking on the busy, crowded streets of downtown, I saw a white man in a business suit shove a black man into the gutter and yell at him because the black man hadn't moved out of his way quickly enough. A crowd of other white people gathered and they were saying awful things. I thought they were going to attack the black man.

Saddened, I moved on quickly. I saw drinking fountains for whites only. And the movie theaters had a separate entrance for black people. There were signs in some stores that said, "No Negroes Allowed."

I remember feeling that they didn't have a chance. I already hated Mississippi and felt sorry for the way the black people were being treated there.

My brother's friends and neighbors thought I was married. Bill and Sue lived in a duplex, and their neighbors were a young couple with no children. When the wife saw that I was pregnant she started right in asking what I wanted, a boy or a girl? When was my husband coming home?

I thought her questions would never stop. I hadn't known the first thing about being married. When I made up stories about my make-believe husband, I would forget what I had said. I tried to be consistent, but it must have been easy to see I was lying.

Fear of being exposed was uppermost in my mind. The people of the South were so different that I could imagine being "tarred and feathered" if they discovered the truth about me.

With all this in mind, I could not bring myself to tell my new doctor that I was not married. Lying to the doctor had not been part of my plan, because I needed to ask him for help with an adoption. Each time I went to the doctor I tried to tell him, and yet I hadn't been able to find the courage.

I discovered that when you lie, you forget the lie, and are forced to lie again to cover the first lie. One lie leads to another. Everyone must have known I was lying about being married. My brother and I talked many times about taking the baby back home to my mother's house.

"Beth, don't do it," he said. "It won't work. You should go

for adoption. Tell the doctor you're not married and ask for his help."

I had always looked up to my brother because he worked hard to get where he was in life. He had the same background as I, so I appreciated his success. We talked about our childhood. He was eleven years older, and I always thought he had looked after me.

He left home when I was nine or ten, so he wasn't there very much while I was growing up. He had always written to me, and we were very close when he was home. I loved him very much. Bill and Sue were good to me and tried to make me feel better. Sue's mother made a maternity smock for me, and Sue cut my hair and gave me a permanent. Of course, I didn't have any money, so they bought me everything I needed.

I valued their love and support and listened when they both advised that I have the baby adopted. My original plan for going to Mississippi had been to have the baby and let it be adopted there. Then I would return to California and resume my life. It had been a nice, neat plan and had sounded so easy, but I couldn't face telling the doctor the truth. What would he think of me? What did I think of me? Not much.

Living the lie was becoming intolerable. If I couldn't even tell the doctor I was unmarried, what was I going to do when the time came to deliver the baby? I would have had to stay at my brother's house with the baby for several weeks before we could travel back home. The situation I had created for myself and my lack of courage was making me sick.

Bill and Sue went to South Carolina for a few days. Wanting the neighbors to stay away, I kept the shades drawn. If they had asked me any more questions, I would have probably broken down and told them the truth. I had to do something. I stayed in bed and prayed for help.

Being alone and depressed, I had time to reflect. I remembered back to December 1945, when Bill and Sue were on their honeymoon and stayed with us. Barely two years ago. We were living in the house that Bill helped mother buy.

Unfortunately, my brother Jack and my stepfather Charlie had talked my mother into selling the house for the money, then we moved to the Housing Project. We had been happy before that, in our own home. Bill and Sue had planned to stay with us only for a month, but Bill had to be hospitalized because of acute mastoiditis in both ears, so their stay was extended for two months. Sue and I became very close and I looked up to her. She was twenty-four and I was eighteen.

I had started working at the Federal Reserve Bank in January 1946, a month after Bill and Sue arrived, and of course I didn't have the proper clothes. Sue and I were the same size and her clothes were beautiful and appropriate for working in a bank.

I remembered how Sue enjoyed dressing me in her clothes and sending me off to work. I felt like a million dollars. When Bill was released from the hospital he had to return to duty, and when they left, Sue gave me two nice outfits, which helped until I could afford more. Sue was encouraging, which gave me confidence. I wanted to be just like her. I had been doing well too, until I let this happen.

I realized I needed help to make my decision. I needed help to feel better about myself. And I needed help to get out of this lie. I could not live like this any longer.

Lying there in the small room in Mississippi, filled with despair, my sobs were deep. With the shades drawn, the sunlight was subdued and I felt a quiet sense of something unusual. I begged God for help. I remember thinking that if I had an audience with God, he would not condemn me. *Please God, help me get home.* With tear-filled eyes and my heart heavy with despair, I imagined I saw a glowing vision standing at the foot of the bed.

By the time Bill and Sue returned from South Carolina, I was despondent and told Bill I had to find a way to get home. My time was running out, I was almost eight months pregnant and I was getting bigger. I could not have the baby in Mississippi and I could not stay any longer.

The only person we knew with money was Uncle Harold. I had to ask him for more help. It was not easy to do, but Bill made the call that evening. I vividly remember standing there, watching and listening to Bill as he explained to Uncle Harold that I needed to get home.

I could see that Bill was embarrassed as he asked our uncle if I could borrow more money. I started crying hysterically, sobbing, walking back and forth, saying I had to get home. I remember Bill motioning me to be quiet as he pointed to the wall: the neighbors would hear me because I was so loud.

Uncle Harold must have heard me too, because he told Bill that he would send the money for me to fly home. I remember my big sobs of relief. I couldn't stop crying. My prayers had been answered. Uncle Harold and Aunt Beth made the arrangements for me to stay at St. Elizabeth's. I flew back, and now that I was safely home in California and in St. Elizabeth's, I felt it was a big relief not to lie anymore.

I could be what I was—a pregnant unmarried woman. Seeing all the other pregnant women just like me was a relief. Not hearing a Southern accent was a relief. I only had my baby to worry about now. I felt my prayers were answered.

I was lucky to be at St. Elizabeth's.

9

MAKING THE BIG DECISION

As the days went by and I felt the peace and quiet, I had more time to think about my decision. I knew that the right thing to do for the child was adoption. I knew that.

As I became familiar with St. Elizabeth's, I started spending time on the third floor. The whole floor was open, except for a glass partition, behind which was the nursery with the babies. A nun was there taking care of them. Part of the big room was used for sewing and the storage of linens. A pay phone was also available for the expectant mothers. The room had a warm feeling.

The babies looked happy and well cared for. I loved watching them. It was hard to believe that I was going to have my baby soon, even though I was sure being kicked a lot. Soon I was standing there and watching the babies every day. I just stood there, staring. One day a nun asked if I planned to give up my child for adoption.

"If you are," she said, "you are only hurting yourself, Justine, looking at the babies every day."

I did it anyway—that is, until I was told again that I was

making a mistake. Then I was told to stay away from the babies for my own good. I realized I was not doing too well.

I remembered that Sister Mary had said to think about going to confession, so I could confess my sins. Maybe that would make me feel better. I had to make my decision soon, as time was running out. One day, after looking at the babies, I called home to talk about the baby and my decision with my mother. I had never really discussed it with her. I was feeling sad and thought she would be able to help me.

When she answered the phone, she didn't give me a chance to talk. She started telling me all her problems, the same old stuff. I started crying and knew I needed to get home to help take care of her.

After we hung up, I hurried, almost running, down to the chapel and got on my knees. I begged God to help my mother until I could get home. I decided to go to confession, too, before I delivered my baby. But I still didn't know what I was going to do.

Suddenly I remembered Halloween night.

Still kneeling there, I thought of my mother and how she had left me alone, eight months pregnant, in that terrible place—a flophouse! I was a young girl in trouble needing my mother's love and understanding, needing help to make the right decision, and when I called her she hadn't even given me a chance to tell her. All she could think about was herself and her problems. She made me feel I had to hurry and get this over with so I could return home to take care of her.

I was crushed.

It was there in the chapel at that moment that I made my decision. I looked up to the altar, still on my knees, and told myself, sobbing, "I have to surrender my baby for adoption. I have to do it. There is no other way."

I could not take my baby to my mother's house, because I knew no one there would really care about us. To do that to my baby would truly be a sin. I would be dooming the baby and myself to a life of the Housing Project and the people who lived there. I would become one of them. *We* would become like them. And I simply could not do that to my child. I made my decision and although I cried and cried, I knew it was right.

The more I knew I had made the right decision, the more depressed I became. I went to confession, but I did not feel any better. I stopped going to the nursery and began to repress my feelings. I knew I could not depend on my family. I knew I had to go to work and repay Uncle Harold all the money I had borrowed. Aunt Beth visited me one day about this time and we met in Mother Superior's office, alone. Aunt Beth was amazed at how I had grown even more in the last three weeks. By this time it was very difficult to get out of a chair.

I could feel her love and support as she said, again, "Bethie, you know you're welcome to come and live with us when this is over. You can go back to the bank and start all over. We would love to have you and so would Harilyn."

After thanking her, I said, "I'd like to do that, Aunt Beth, but I know I have to go back home and find a job in Oakland, to help my mother. But I'll come over to visit you on weekends, and please tell Uncle Harold I'll pay him back."

When I was alone in my room and opened the suitcase Aunt Beth had brought me, I had a flood of memories from another life as I saw all my clothes. I hoped they would fit me again when all this was over. Sobbing to myself, I was determined that I would work hard and stand on my own two feet. I would get on with my life to accomplish the goals I had set for myself. I knew I needed to work hard to be able to leave my mother's house as soon as I could. There was no way I could, or would, take my baby there.

At about this time I acquired a roommate. Her name was June, and she had a mature businesswoman's look about her. She was probably thirty years old. She didn't have very long to go before her due date either. I liked her and felt comfortable with her. I vaguely remember her telling me that the nuns were concerned about me and felt that I should not be alone. Since I had stopped going to the third floor and staring at the babies, the nuns must have noticed that I stayed in my room most of the time.

They probably knew I was very depressed and thought it would be good for me to have a roommate. June and I talked about adoption and I told her of my decision. She was going to have her child adopted as well. At dinner that evening, I told the others at my table of my decision. We were all going to do the same. Nancy, the expectant mother who had the longest to go before her due date, assisted Nurse Tess and helped the doctor with the births. She told us what happens.

She said the rule was that we would be given ether and put out completely during the childbirth. The nuns felt we should not remember what it was like to have a baby. Someday, if we had other children, it would be like having our first child. Nancy went on to explain that even though we were allowed to see our babies for the two weeks that we had to stay there after delivery, the nuns strongly advised against it.

I guess they felt it would be easier on us and we would forget all about it sooner if we did not see our babies. Hard as it was, most of the new mothers followed their advice. We were constantly told to put it all behind us, not to think about it, keep it a secret, forget it and get on with your life. Everything would be all right and we would be happy. The baby would be happy and would have a good life with a loving mother and father in a nice house with plenty of money.

I was going to have a baby. I was going to be a mother, but I was not going to know what it was like when I was having the baby. It must have been then that I became the "good little girl." The good little girl who follows all the advice she is given.

They had said everything would be peaches and cream. I kept telling myself that, over and over again. I stuffed and buried and buried and stuffed and everything stayed buried.

10

I HAVE A SON I CAN'T KEEP

When I woke up on December 3, I was concerned. I was late, two days past my due date. I lay there, large and uncomfortable. Although it was difficult to get out of bed, I managed to get up, dress myself and go to breakfast.

I no longer walked, I waddled. And when I waddled, I leaned backwards because I was so top-heavy. I felt exhausted from the constant action of my baby. After breakfast it was a struggle to clear the tables. I was anxious to lie down. I was getting worried; it had better happen soon. I realized that in my four weeks at St. Elizabeth's, I had not been examined once.

As I climbed onto the bed, I said to myself, "Justine, you passed your due date of December first. What's going on?" I smiled as I put my hands on my stomach. It felt strange to have so much movement going on in there.

I started feeling sad again. I knew Justine and the baby would be leaving me soon. Deep in my secret heart I would miss them. I wanted to say something to both of them.

Deep in my secret heart,
There is a Tiny Soul,
Waiting to come out.

Are you ready to come out,
And leave me?

Please don't come out,
And leave me.

You have to,
I know,
It's nearly time.

We'll have to say good-by.
I'll never see you,
I'll never know you.
I'll never forget you,
My Tiny Soul.

I tried and tried,
To find a way.

I'm sorry I got you into this.
I love you, my Tiny Soul,
And I always will.

I don't know how long I had been lying on my bed when Nancy came in.

"Justine, are you all right? Michele has started labor. Will you walk the halls with her? You've passed your due date, so maybe walking the halls will bring your baby on."

I struggled to get up.

"Sure," I said, moving like a snail, "I'll walk the halls with Michele."

We found Michele and started walking, Nancy on one side of her and me on the other. What a picture we made as

65

we waddled along. When someone started into labor, the news traveled fast and we all got excited for the mother-to-be. Her time at St. Elizabeth's was coming to an end. She could put it all behind her and get on with her life. Just like they promised us.

I was totally taken by surprise when suddenly my water broke, and I let out a yelp, close to the activity room. Nancy knew at once what had happened.

"Justine, you're starting. Now we have two of you in labor."

When the expectant mothers heard our excitement and laughter in the hallway, they came running out of the activity room to see what was going on.

"Michele has been in labor," Nancy told them, "and now Justine is in labor too. I wonder who'll deliver first."

She made it sound like a contest, a race. We were just outside the entrance to the isolated wing of St. Elizabeth's, the off-limits section where the mothers who had already delivered were confined. The isolated wing was like a hospital, with another set of double doors, only smaller. It definitely was off-limits to the expectant mothers. After a woman delivered, we never saw her again.

It was all very exciting as I walked through the doors, knowing I was entering another world. From that point on, though, it's all very vague. I remember Tess the Nurse and Nancy looking down at me, so I must have been on the delivery table. I remember them saying something about ether.

That is all I can recall about the birth of my son on December 3, 1947, at around three in the afternoon. I don't even know who told me he was a boy, or that he weighed about eight pounds. It was all so unnatural to have a child that way. Not to know the exact time of delivery or weight of the baby felt so unfinished, as if they wanted us to feel we hadn't had a child at all. As if none of this had happened.

Nancy had been right. I still didn't know what it was like to have a baby. When I came out from under the ether, I was on my stomach, of all things. I was sobbing and saying over and over, "I have a boy, and I can't keep him."

I remember someone telling me that Michele was still in labor, so I had delivered first. Somehow it didn't seem to matter now. The next morning when the nurses came to take care of me, I had my first chance to see that I was in a hospital ward with five beds. I was rather surprised that this part of St. Elizabeth's was so different and that I hadn't even known it existed.

Our meals were served on hospital trays and the food was good. The nurses came to take care of us every day, to bind our breasts and make sure we were healing properly. We were treated well.

There had been two other mothers like me and two empty beds and we had been told not to go beyond the double doors so the mothers-to-be would not have contact with us. The three of us mothers were in various stages of depression, crying a lot, and I'm sure the nuns did not want us around the other women, who would realize how sad we were.

I felt fortunate that again my bed was by one of the windows, so I would have the sunlight and be able to look across to the other wing of the building and up one floor to the windows of the nursery, where my one-day-old baby boy was being cared for by the nuns.

Later that same day Michele had delivered her baby. Lying in my bed, I watched her being placed in the bed next to mine. Soon after that, Sister Mary came to see me. She needed to know what name I wanted for my son.

"I want to name him Harold, after my uncle."

"I'm sorry, Justine," Sister Mary said, "but Harold is not a saint's name. You have to name your son after a saint."

I was disappointed that I wasn't even allowed to choose the name of my baby. Grabbing a name out of the air, I said, "Oh, ah, John. Yes, John."

"That's a fine name for your son, Justine. You have a fine

healthy boy and he will be placed with a good family and have a good life."

She patted my shoulder, and continued, "You're doing the right thing, Justine, giving up your son. Now you can put it all behind you. Forget it and get on with your life."

As the nurses were taking care of me, they informed me that my son had lots of black hair. All the babies in our family have had lots of black hair. He was cute and chubby. My mother had told me I had been cute and chubby. I was relieved that he was healthy and normal. Now a nice family would want to adopt him. But I was still sad. I missed his kicking.

Every day the nurses would tell me a little more about my son. He smiled and was a good baby; he wasn't crying all the time. I desperately wanted to see him and hold him, but I knew if I did, it would be harder still. As I lay in bed for those first few days, the words, "Get on with your life" kept going through my mind. Then I would turn my head and look at the nursery windows and cry, hoping I had made the right decision.

About that time I decided to write a letter to Henry, telling him that he had a son and although I didn't know for sure what he looked like, I described the baby as best I could. I wanted to make him feel bad.

Once, I was awakened in the middle of the night. I sat up in bed and watched a young girl I knew to be sixteen being placed in bed after delivering her baby. As she came out from under the ether, she was crying, calling over and over for her mommy.

I remember thinking that she was still a little kid. No wonder she was calling for her mommy. Now she was a mommy herself. I felt angry. I thought, *It takes two to make a baby. Where are the men and boys who are the other half of this situation?* It seemed so easy for men. They didn't have to suffer in the least for their actions.

The girl's name was Suzy—her false name, that is. She

was a pretty blond with freckles and she looked like a cheer-leader. We all had our stories, and now our sadness. I thought it was very unfair.

A special privilege had been granted to us mothers, a free night to the outside world to attend a movie. It was frightening, but the four of us who were healed enough talked each other into going. Thank God, Aunt Beth had brought my clothes and, thank God, they fit. I remember the relief I felt as I tried on the best dress I had. I must have borrowed a coat.

Walking out through the big double doors was actually frightening. We had to take a bus from Geary Street and transfer to a streetcar on Market Street to get to the Paramount Theater. I was cold and nervous standing on Market Street waiting for the streetcar.

What if someone from my old job at the bank walked past and saw me? What would I say? I would have had to make up more lies and I wanted to be through with lies. The four of us had a good time and felt free again. We didn't look any different from anyone else. No one would know that we were from that home for unwed mothers. We did feel privileged and happy that our ordeal was almost over.

I have absolutely no memory of the movie.

For the few days remaining before my time to leave St. Elizabeth's, I sat and looked up at the windows of the nursery. I followed the advice of the nuns and was the good little girl. I never saw my son. In those two weeks after I gave birth, I learned how to hide all my feelings and emotions about my son, about being his mother and the fact that I had surrendered him for adoption.

When it came time to leave St. Elizabeth's, I kept telling myself I was doing the right thing. I hoped my son would have a good life and would be happy. He would never know me, or know I was his mother. I had to trust God to keep him safe.

As I walked slowly through the big double doors, leaving St. Elizabeth's, I said to my son, John:

> Deep in my secret heart
> Where your Tiny Soul was
>
> I will place a part of me
> That belongs to you forever.

I kept hearing the words, "Put it all behind you, Beth." With my head held high, but with a breaking heart, I walked down the stairs. Being a good little girl, I buried it all and went on with my life.

11

BACK TO REALITY—1993

Opening my eyes the next morning, I'm jolted awake, wide awake. Have I been dreaming? Did I meet my son last night? Feeling unreal, I realize it's not a dream. Mike is alive! My son is alive and I met him for the first time in my life. It really happened!

I almost need to pinch myself to know that it's me with this wonderful new event. Less than twenty-four hours ago I didn't have a son. Now I do. He's a grown man. He found me, after searching for five years! Me, his mother! Smiling, I think, he's great and so is his wife, Linda. We had such a good time last night. I feel bewildered as I try to put this all together.

I remembered Justine. I hadn't thought about her in many years. Can she be me? Did all of that really happen to me? I have always thought of Justine as someone else, not me. But Justine was real too; not a dream. She has been tucked away in my heart for forty-five years. Poor Justine, she deserves to rest now. Her work is finished.

Starting to cry as I think about all this, and not wanting to wake Chuck, I quietly get out of bed and grab my robe.

Walking down the stairs and looking around my home, I notice again that everything feels so different, so peaceful and calm, yet it is all the same. I sit at the table in a trance, waiting for my first cup of coffee, still in a state of shock that this could be happening.

My world is changing.

Has changed.

I'm afraid to believe this. If I let myself believe and it's not true, could I handle another loss? I'm gasping for air. I think I had better slow down to make sure last night really happened. Filled with an overpowering fear, I think, *What if it's not real? What if it's not him?*

On the other hand, he looked happy and was excited to see me. He certainly had plenty of proof in his file. It's me, all right. I'm his mother and he is the little boy I gave birth to. It's him; it's just that I can't believe my good fortune that he actually wanted to find me.

He didn't act angry or full of resentment for my walking away from him. I still can't believe I did that. How terrible. Maybe today, now that Mike has met me and is thinking about it, he is having second thoughts and hates me for what I did. *Please, God, don't let that be true.*

Realizing the gravity of my actions forty-five years ago strikes me hard. I ask myself, *How could I have given up my child? I walked away from him and gave him to someone else. How could I have done that?*

Maybe I'll have a chance on Sunday to explain why I didn't keep him. I need to say something to him about that. But I can't even explain it to myself yet. Thinking about last night, sitting next to Mike in the restaurant and not remembering anything about the papers from his file, some of the pieces of the puzzle are starting to fit together.

I remember now: the infant I was holding in the picture, was my nephew, Jim, born twenty days after Mike. My brother-in-law was the only one in the family with a camera and it was his child I was holding. The picture was the only recent one I had of myself at that time. I guess I wanted Mike's parents to see what I looked like.

But what about the picture of my brother Jack? Vaguely I remember thinking that the adoptive parents should have a picture of a male from my family. It might have been my mother's suggestion. It had to be me who sent the pictures to attorney Philip Adams, but I can't remember doing it.

Sitting here with my coffee, thinking about everything that happened last night, more pieces of the puzzle are fitting together. After receiving the phone call from St. Elizabeth's in February 1948 and knowing that my son was still there after three months, I must have told Aunt Beth and Uncle Harold about Mr. Adams and that I was going to ask for his help in finding a good home for Mike. Aunt Beth and Uncle Harold must have sent Philip Adams the list of expenses and birth-father Henry's letters.

They might have thought that the attorney would help pressure Henry for some financial help. I know from reading Henry's letters that my aunt and uncle did. I vaguely remember something about that when I was in Mississippi, but I'm sure I didn't know there had been letters.

Seeing Henry's letters last night had added to the shock for me. They were from a different world. It's difficult to deal with something that has been so deeply buried for forty-five years. I remember how I felt about myself then, and my broken heart for what I had to do.

Chuck comes downstairs for breakfast, startling me out of my preoccupation with the past, bringing me back to today. With a big smile he sits at the table holding his coffee.

"Well, Beth, you must be really happy about Mike's finding you. I like him and Linda. He seems like a very nice guy."

"I am happy Chuck, but I still can't believe something like this could happen. Through the years, whenever I thought of him, it was an instant fleeting thought, always on his birthday, and all through the Vietnam war years, he was out there. I didn't have a face for him, I couldn't visualize him. He was just—out there, somewhere. I thought I would never know, and now he's here."

"He sure wanted to find you," he said. "You must feel great. It's like a miracle."

"It *is* a miracle. I'm sure glad to know him, to see what he looks like, to hear his voice. He's nice. In fact, I think he's great. In my wildest dreams I never thought this would happen. He sounds very much like my brother Bill."

Chuck mentions that Mike reminds him of Bill too. In fact, we both think that it's rather stunning, the resemblance and his mannerisms. Sitting here and hearing Chuck say that, I have a feeling I recognize as peaceful. Yes, a calmness is how to describe what I feel. Chuck is enjoying this new world too, and seems to notice the difference. He mentions that we should tell our family and friends about Mike and his finding me.

I have to face the facts. This is too wonderful for words, but how do I handle it? My big secret will have to be told to everyone. To tell people of my own generation will be very hard. With my approval, Chuck starts calling our friends. He tells them about the Special Delivery letter. He sounds so happy that people are instantly happy for us.

Everyone is shocked. Some say they have goose bumps; others even cry. Chuck tells them all about Mike and his search, about our having two more granddaughters. He jokes about my being the grandmother of a twenty-five-year-old.

Watching him beaming and truly happy about this, I feel very grateful. I appreciate how he is taking all this. He has a stepson now, and he is genuinely happy for me. He is enjoying himself, and I think he's doing a great job of answering everyone's questions.

I keep giving him the high sign to be sure he tells everyone that I was engaged back then and that I told him about Mike before we married. As if it makes any difference. But it does to me. I'm having a hard time with this, I realize, but those are the facts. So I sit here watching Chuck go through the list, because I can't face telling anyone myself, not yet.

Most of our family had known for years about my having a child and placing him for adoption. They are delighted to hear the news that he has found me. In fact, they all cry with happiness for me. I feel unbelievably happy. A new kind of happiness, a wonderful blessed event.

The next day, calling some of my cousins is difficult and embarrassing for me. One cousin, my age, tells me she had known for years and never had a problem with it. What does that mean? Does it mean that everyone else had a problem with it? I don't know.

I call another cousin, about twelve years younger than me, who has a younger sister. She tells me they had known for years too. Her mother used me as an example when they were growing up: "Remember what happened to Bethie."

I know all my cousins are very happy for me, but to learn that they knew for years is shocking. I feel exposed. I had thought no one knew, but I should have realized how fast a scandal travels.

My cousin Harilyn is delighted with the good news; she is thrilled for me. Harilyn knew about the baby in 1948. She remembers feeling so abandoned when I didn't come home from Mississippi. With all the whispering going on by her mother, she demanded to know why I hadn't come back. Aunt Beth finally told her the truth. Harilyn remembers exactly what her response to her mother was.

"What? Why would she do a dumb thing like getting pregnant?"

We both laughed.

"I guess that was a typical response for a twelve-year-old who felt abandoned and left out of everything," Harilyn said.

"Gosh, Harilyn, I never even thought how you might feel," I told her. "I'm sorry you felt bad. I know how you looked up to me and you must have been disappointed in your idol. But," I told her, "you were right, it was a really dumb thing to let happen to me. When I think of how naive I was, I can't believe it."

Saying good-by, Harilyn tells me she couldn't be any happier for me, especially since Susan, one of her favorite people, had died.

Working up the courage, I next call one of my oldest friends, Doris, a co-worker from Crocker Bank, where I went to work about six weeks after Mike was born. We had been very close friends; in fact, Doris was the one who encouraged me to have a big wedding when Chuck and I were married. She and I shopped for my wedding gown on our lunch hour. I even borrowed Doris' Juliet cap and veil.

I still remember how I felt in that gorgeous gown. Doris and her husband were both in our wedding, and the four of us had been very close friends.

"I didn't know you at all, did I?" is her first reaction.

Feeling let down, I tell her, "No, you didn't." Then I quickly add, "But, yes, you really did. That was me you worked with."

When I tell Doris my story and what had happened just before we met and worked together, and of my decision to have Mike adopted, she says she recalls how things were in 1947.

"It must have been terrible for you, Beth. I remember how society was in those days. I remember that we both had a difficult childhood, and what it was like for you living with your family in the Project. You and I were both determined to have a better life. Remember, you were trying to move into the Blue Triangle when you met Chuck? Imagine, the Blue Triangle, a hotel for women." With a smile in her voice, she adds, "Unheard of in society today."

"The Blue Triangle," I exclaimed—something else I had forgotten.

"Yes," I said. "I had a personal interview and I was accepted. Of course, they didn't know about me, or they

76

wouldn't have accepted me. I remember it seemed expensive to live there, but it would have been worth it."

"I'm glad society is different today," Doris says.

I'm feeling better as she adds, "Beth, I'm so happy for you. It's wonderful. I feel like crying, especially after your losing Susan." Saying good-by and thanking her, I hang up. Then I start crying.

After talking to Doris, I remember when Crocker Bank hired me. I was sent to the bank's doctor in San Francisco for a physical examination. I sat in the doctor's waiting room, thinking over and over, *He's going to know, he's going to know I just had a baby. Maybe he won't and I won't have to tell him.*

After the examination, as I sat in the doctor's office, I remember he was looking down, reading my chart. He could see that I wasn't married. Then he looked at me.

"Did you recently have a child?"

Sitting across from his desk, my hand flew to my mouth to stop a sob, and I cried with a choked gush of words, "Yes, the father and I were engaged. But he was already married, I think. I had to have the baby adopted."

I was so afraid the bank would find out and I wouldn't get the job. The doctor looked at me with sympathy, sighed and said, "Don't worry, I won't put it in your record. No one will know." Then I was really crying, thanking him with gratitude and shame.

Now, as I sit by the phone after talking to Doris, my mind goes back to that time.

When my mother received the phone call from St. Elizabeth's in February 1948 and learned that Mike was still there, she called me at work. Frantic, I called June, the girl who had been my roommate, and she arranged for me to meet her attorney in San Francisco.

I remember asking my mother, "What am I going to do? I just started working at the bank last month. How on earth am I going to be able to take a day off to go to San Francisco?"

My fear of the bank and the people I worked with finding out I had just had a baby out of wedlock filled me with panic.

"Beth," my mother had said emphatically, "you just tell them that you need the day off to take care of some personal business in San Francisco."

Somehow, my mother was right. I took the day off and met with Philip Adams. A few months later, I received a phone call at work from him. Our home phone had been disconnected because of nonpayment, so Mr. Adams could not reach me there. Embarrassed, I felt that everyone in the office knew I was talking to a lawyer.

Someone might ask why I would need a lawyer.

Mr. Adams informed me that there were papers I needed to sign. Could I return to San Francisco to sign them? Panic again. I told him I didn't see how I could take another day off for personal business as I was still a new employee. He must have heard the fear in my voice and known I had difficulty talking to him from work. He told me he would drive to Oakland the next day and that he would park in front of the bank at a certain time.

I thanked him, but now I felt even more fear. How could I explain sitting in his car on my coffee break in front of Crocker Bank, on the busy corner of 13th and Franklin Streets, right across the street from the Oakland Tribune building? Of course, as I sat in his car signing papers, a group of my co-workers passed on their way to the coffee shop and smiled at me. I blushed with guilt and looked away.

For many months after Mike was born, I still lived with the shame of being an unwed mother, and the terrible fear of being exposed. By August of 1948, when I went to San Francisco to sign the final adoption papers,

I was a proven employee and found the courage to ask for the time off.

How could I have forgotten Philip Adams's name? He had been extremely kind to me, driving all the way to Oakland because our phone had been disconnected. I was embarrassed at the time, but all I could say was thank you. He never did charge me. And now he's an older gentlemen, and he simply handed my file to my son, after forty-five years. Remarkable.

Just two nights ago, sitting in the restaurant, I remember Mike commenting in a rather surprised voice, "The telephone was in your name? Beth Heath?"

He was talking about 1948 phone records. He sure had found out a lot about me. I had completely forgotten that.

"Of course," I answered matter-of-factly. "I was the only one in the household who was working."

So I guess it wasn't long after Philip Adams tried to reach me that the phone was put in my name. Remembering all this is sad and feels as if these memories don't belong to me. I'm finding it difficult for someone of my age and times to remember being poor and the shame of having a child out of wedlock. I have to admit I broke the rules and paid dearly.

But the miracle of having my son find me after forty-five years is well worth it. In fact, I feel like standing on a mountain top and shouting to the world that my son has found me. "I have a son!"

When I call our daughter Linda and tell her about our meeting Mike and his wife and how nice he is and that he looks so much like Bill, she is excited and anxious to meet him. As we discuss the planned Sunday reunion, Linda tells me, "Guinevere and I will arrive on Saturday to help, so don't worry, Mom. I can just imagine the shock you must feel. I feel it too and I can't wait to meet him."

Needing to stay focused, I clean everything in sight. My

mind tells me over and over this really isn't happening. God! My son will be walking through our front door. I'm in shock with the impact of all that has happened. He wanted to find me. It is beyond belief. Thank God, it was not beyond belief for Mike. I'm thrilled and overwhelmed.

Mike and Beth

Beth on her 70th birthday.

Uncle Harold and Aunt Beth in 1928.

St. Elizabeth's Home for unwed mothers
big double doors and stairs.

Beth and Chuck—just married August 21, 1949

Chuck and Beth in their yard.

Mike—First Holy Commu-
nion day—probably 7 or 8.

Son, Mike, 17 years old.

My daughter Susan, left and
Mike's daughter Kim, right.

Susan and Linda 1957.

Susan and Linda 1985.

*Above: Chuck, Linda,
Susan, and Beth 1959.*

Right: Daughter Linda

*My 55th birthday September, 1982
L to R: Susan, Beth, Linda, and Chuck*

Mike and his daughter, Kim, on the day of our family reunion, August 15, 1993.

Mike and Beth—first picture, 5 minutes after meeting in parking lot, August, 11, 1993.

Reunion, August 15, 1993. L to R: Mike, wife Linda in front of Mike, sister Linda next to Mike on couch, Mike's daughter Kim, our Linda's daughter Guinevere, birthmother Beth, Beth's husband Chuck.

Susan's children, . . . Stephanie, left, Greg, right, Beth, middle.

Linda's daughter, Guinevere, left and Susan's daughter, Stephanie, right.

12

MEETING THE FAMILY

By the time Sunday arrives, I'm a basket case, beside myself with self-doubt. What will I wear, how should I look? Should I dress up? I don't think so. Trying on everything in my closet, I have a pile of clothes heaped on the bed. Again I choose jeans and a white blouse.

Mike isn't sure what time they will be arriving. With my daughter Linda and granddaughter Guinevere helping, we're ready by one o'clock. We're excited, not knowing what to expect. Linda is anxious to meet her brother. She suggests we have an assortment of cold cuts and salad because we have no idea how long they can stay or how many are coming.

"Mother, don't try to cook a meal. You can't spend the day in the kitchen. With cold cuts, it won't matter."

She is right, as usual. We are as ready as we can get and so anxious that it's hard to wait. By the time Mike and his wife arrive, I'm trembling again and taking deep breaths.

The first couple of minutes are awkward for all of us. Seeing Mike look at his sister, and Linda looking at her brother for the first time, fills me with an exhilarating joy. They hug and start talking and discover a kinship. I love looking at them. I cannot stop thinking how Susan, the daughter we lost, would love this moment, meeting her brother, as Linda is.

Mike mentions that his daughter Kim will be arriving a little later. Seana and her new husband Glen have already left for their honeymoon. Mike and his wife make themselves at home, and we all try to relax. With plenty to talk about, the awkwardness soon disappears. Watching everyone, I realize how happy I am to see my two children getting to know each other.

When Kim arrives, I can't believe my eyes. I hear Chuck draw in his breath, stunned. I see this beautiful girl and I am looking at my new granddaughter who resembles Susan so much that she could be her daughter. Transfixed, my hands fly to cover my face. I have to turn away for fear I will burst out in tears. I hear myself say, "Oh, my God, you're beautiful!" as I throw my arms around her.

I think I overwhelm her, but she hugs me back. She feels so familiar, as if she belongs to me. I don't want to let her go. Who would ever believe that this child would look so much like Susan—the same size, the same coloring, the same shape face, all except for the color of her eyes and no dimple.

Not wanting to overpower Kim, I don't mention the resemblance. I look at Chuck and see he is as stirred as I am by this breathtaking event. We both glance at our daughter, Linda. The look on her face tells us her experience was as jolting as ours. Mike tells me later that he was watching my face when Kim walked through our front door. For him, his long years of searching were worth it at that moment, when he saw how deep my emotions were.

His dream was to find his mother, so his mother could see his wonderful daughters. Of course, he had no way of knowing that one of his daughters would have such a strong resemblance to our daughter, Susan, another miracle. How many miracles am I allowed in one lifetime?

After a while Linda and Guinevere bring out some of our

family albums. Not wanting to force anyone to look at them, they quietly put them on the coffee table. Mike's wife picks up one of the albums and the two Lindas are having fun as our Linda points out pictures of herself and Susan as children. Kim is sitting there with a look of amazement on her face, saying, "There's my mouth," or "I have the same lips," as she sees first one picture of Susan, then another.

They're as fascinated, as we are. Every so often Mike's wife reaches over and shows him a picture with a knowing look. I'm sitting across the room watching and feeling I'm in Never-never Land.

What must it be like for Mike to find his mother and sister? It must be equally strange for Kim to meet a grandmother, an aunt and a cousin. To be sitting in a strange house, looking at pictures of your new extended family and seeing so many resemblances that you had not known existed a few days ago.

No wonder they are utterly engrossed. I'm watching all this and can't believe my eyes. Then Mike asks a few questions about St. Elizabeth's and when he was born.

I realize that Chuck, Linda and Guinevere had not heard any of this either. I'm embarrassed, feeling I'm on center stage. I trip over my words and nothing is coming out right. When I start to go into some details about my childhood and family, I can see that Chuck is embarrassed for me. What am I doing? Trying to justify why I had to give Mike up for adoption? I don't know. I'm completely rattled.

Telling Mike and his wife about Mississippi is also the first time my family is hearing any of my story. Even though they knew about Mike, I had never told them the details. Mike wants to know all about me and I want to know all about him, too, but there are too many people around, and not enough time.

Trying to fill Mike in on some of our family history, I tell him that my father was a Southern gentleman from Kentucky, who wore a derby hat and spats. Surprised, Linda says,

"Mom, I don't remember your telling us that about your father. He actually wore a derby and spats?"

"Yes, he did," I answer. "In fact, I have a picture of him somewhere with his derby hat, spats and even a cane. When he came to California, he became a streetcar conductor in Oakland, and that's how my mother met him. She must have been a passenger on his streetcar many times. According to my Uncle Raleigh, a streetcar conductor was considered poor white trash in the South."

I could see that everyone was interested. Then I said, "I just remembered. I have a copy of the family history. My father's brother Raleigh went to Kentucky in 1935 and explored the Heath family tree. I'll see if I can find it."

As I run up the stairs, I wonder where it could be. Good, I found it, for a change just where I thought it was. Going back downstairs, I hand the ten-page family history to Mike.

"You wanted to know about your family? Well, here's two hundred years of history on my father's side. It goes back to before the American Revolution, in the deep South, where my father's family were aristocratic Southerners and slave owners. They all had very Southern names. It's funny to read, especially written in 1935 by my very Southern uncle."

The family history hadn't meant much to me because I had no respect for my father or the Southerners of that era. Telling Mike, who is almost a stranger, about people with whom he has a direct biological link feels unreal. He looks overwhelmed at this point. He must be in the same fog and as confused as I am.

I notice everyone looking at me and telling each other how good I look. I can't remember ever receiving so much attention and again I feel like a movie star. Mike, Linda and their daughter Kim seem delighted with all of us. My daughter notices I'm rattled and suggests that she, with the help of Guinevere and Kim, take care of serving the food. What a thrill to see the three of them in the kitchen together.

While waiting, Chuck shows Mike around the house and

yard. Mike's wife and I have a few minutes together on the patio. She tells me many things about Mike—how he will never go away. I could count on that. He is that kind of a person.

I'm impressed by her sincerity and don't know how to respond, so I say, "I just thought of something. I've never had a daughter-in-law before. I guess you are my daughter-in-law."

"I sure am," Linda says with a smile on her face.

Linda is open and friendly and very happy for both Mike and me. I appreciate how much she wants me to know that Mike is a sincere person. I have the same sensation I had earlier, of everything feeling pure and clean, of everything coming together. I can almost understand what is happening to me.

"Mike's parents," I say with some difficulty, "must be wonderful people, because it is obvious that he had all the love he needed as a child."

Standing there on the patio, it was disturbing to face the fact that I had given my child to them. What must it be like to have a mother who gave you away, to wonder all your life who your real mother is and what she is like? I never thought how it must feel to not know where you came from, to not know your family's history.

I feel embarrassed again, and again I want to tell Mike why I did what I did.

He certainly seems happy he found me. He acts as if he likes what he has found in our family—his family, too, now. When Linda and my two granddaughters call us to the dining room, I'm surprised. Here I have my new son, his wife and my new granddaughter for dinner for the first time, and with all my fine china and linen available, we end up with a vinyl tablecloth. Mayonnaise and mustard jars are on the table, with knives sticking out of them.

If I were trying to impress my new son and his family, mayonnaise and mustard jars with knives sticking out was definitely not what I had in mind. When I mention it, I see that no one cares but me. While we are eating, Mike's wife points out that he does not like vegetables, anything green. It is as if she is telling his mother that he has been naughty. It becomes a joke. Mike looks sheepish and tries to explain. I love vegetables and I say so, but tell him it's okay.

Then I ask, "But you do like asparagus and artichokes, don't you?"

"No," he answers, with an apologetic look.

"Well, Mike, you should have included that information in your Special Delivery letter," I say in a falsely mocking tone. "If I had known you didn't like your vegetables, well . . . I don't know. . . . Maybe I wouldn't have made the call."

What fun we were having, laughing with the newfound excitement of being together. We start comparing many things we have in common, enjoying the sense of familiarity.

Guinevere is showing Kim, her new cousin, the house; they go upstairs to see other family pictures. I'm thrilled to see them together and notice how proud Guin is. Guin is seventeen and I had thought she was my oldest grandchild, but now I also have a twenty-five and a twenty-one-year-old. Amazing. I'm bursting with happiness.

Before the evening is over, Kim and I have a few moments alone upstairs. Looking at more pictures, she mentions with a fond look, "I've often wondered what I will be like when I'm older. Now, after meeting you, I know. I'm so happy to know you."

After seeing her strong resemblance to Susan herself, she asks, "I hope it's not sad for you, that I look so much like Susan?"

"Oh, Kim," I answer, feeling close to her, "your looking like Susan is a blessing, a gift from Heaven. But it is you we are all thrilled to know and to have in our family."

I feel myself loving this lovely young woman—my granddaughter. When I hug her, it's as if I have known her all of her life. The emotional pull is deep and strong. She is part of me and we are connected; we belong to each other.

Suddenly the day of our reunion is over. It's time for them to leave and I need to say something. I need to explain to Mike why I did what I did, forty-five years ago.

But first, I need to explain it to myself.

13

LOVE AND EUPHORIA

Roaming the house all day Monday, not able to focus on anything, my mind won't stop asking the question, *When will I see him again?* I realize we didn't make any sort of a date and I need the security of knowing. Is he disappointed? He seemed happy.

I wish I could have talked to him in private, but we did not have one minute alone. Of course, everyone was watching us, continuously, because they were all so happy for us and this miracle. I needed to explain, and I had no chance. I am still shocked and embarrassed by what our daughter Linda said this morning, before she went home. We were standing in our kitchen and I was still going on and on about Mike. She looked at me and smiled.

"Mom, don't you know what's happening to you? You're falling in love."

My mouth flew open.

"Linda!"

I was aghast at her saying such a shocking thing in front of her father and Guinevere, and I could feel my face turning red. This isn't a romance. This is mother and child. He just happens to be forty-five years old.

Tuesday, at about four in the morning, not being able to sleep, I decide to get out of bed and go downstairs to start writing. My mind is racing with all kinds of new, wonderful, fearful thoughts. I remember that after Susan died, when my mind was scattered in all directions, writing helped me put my thoughts in focus and helped me understand. With Susan, I lost a child to death. Now, to have a child that I gave away come back into my life—there are no words to describe it.

Sitting here with my first cup of coffee, my notebook and pen in my hand, now what? What do I write? I've never had this experience before. Then it comes to me: a letter.

> Dear Michael, Dear John:
>
> I've never written your name before. I've never written you a letter before. I'm trying to figure this whole thing out—my feelings, that is. Right now my strongest feeling is major fear!
>
> Fear that I'll wake up from this wonderful dream. Fear of something started, but not fulfilled. Fear of my letting go of emotions of forty-five years and of being so exposed that I can never recover.
>
> Right now there is a great force moving within me. I can feel it and I'm afraid. Please don't walk away before I can put this all in perspective. What's stirring in me is a long-buried love—first time for that word.
>
> It's there, I can feel it bubbling to the surface. I haven't cried yet. I really need to. This is so wonderful, it must be true. I can't believe anyone can be like you, Mike. Your search seemed so intense. Your yearning to find your mother, any mother, but your real mother didn't have to be me. Your yearning was for that mother.
>
> You seem to have been loving that mother for years. Now that's me. How come? I know without a doubt you are the little boy I gave life to. I hope you can forgive me.

Thank you for your search and being the kind of person to do it. Thank you forever for letting me see you.

I'm crying now, crying at last.

I'm crying and I can't stop. Please don't go away now. I'm crying just the same as I did for Susan. You have unleashed a ton of tears. Susan is mixed in there too.

Mike, you couldn't know what you have done, but now that you have done it, please stick around for a while and let me get to know you. I'm sorry I had to do what I did when you were born.

I'm smart enough to know that I can't and won't hang onto you and become (I can't find the right word) an obsessed, crazed mother. Don't worry about that.

I am your birth-mother. Your other mother is your real mother in my eyes. She raised you and loves you with all her heart and soul. You were raised with unconditional love, a true mother's love. She did that for you. Not me.

But I thank her forever. One thing I'm really grateful for is that you're a fine human being, and your adoptive mother did that.

I feel such relief. You're alive. You're handsome. I can see you are a loving person that I can be proud of. For the rest of my life, no matter what develops between us (and it's up to you), I will at least have had a chance to see you and touch you, that little boy of many years ago.

I'll be able to handle it. I hope we can have a lasting relationship and that I can earn your respect and love. On Sunday at our house, I just wanted to look at you, but of course I couldn't just do that. Still, I could see and feel a look in your eyes that was so forceful and compelling.

I know without a doubt that you are my . . . —I can't say the word yet. I need more reassurance. I can't be too exposed.

Having a son and giving him up, having a daughter and losing her, and now you find me after forty-five years— I feel I am the luckiest woman on earth. What a wonderful feeling. Thanks.

The next day, having read this letter, I realize it really expressed my feelings and helped to keep my mind focused, while trying to deal with so many new and unfamiliar emotions. So I'll write another letter today.

Dear Mike:

I must call you. I need to talk to you. I need to know where this is going. I need to be reassured it's going forward. Slow is okay, but forward. I need to feel safe.

I have many years ahead of me to protect and keep my head straight; therefore, I need to do this right.

One week ago right now I didn't know you. To be very selfish, I need to hold you and tell you, "Hello, welcome to the world." I never got to do that.

. . . I called you just now and, Heaven on earth, we talked.

You are everything I could ever hope for. You said all the right words, right tone of voice, right softness, right everything. Thank you.

You let me talk and you listened. You heard and I heard. It was delicious. I can feel myself falling in love. A real miracle.

Each day, after reading what I have written to Mike, I feel overwhelmed with deep emotions that are totally bewildering. Because I never experienced anything like this before, writing seems to be the only way to stay focused, so here I go, pouring my heart out, again.

Dear Mike:

I feel so good. Here is my heart, take it. I'm handing it to you, freely. Don't drop it or break it, please. It's the only heart I have and it already has some cracks.

You seem like such a gentle man and I hear so much kindness in your voice. So I shouldn't worry about my heart. I'm glad I'm young for my age. I think, feel and act young. It's just a fact. I didn't have much to do with it.

I must confess, now that you have arrived in my life, I'm really glad you didn't find otherwise. I've never had trouble getting older, until I reached sixty-five. I had been very depressed, wondering how I would fill up the next twenty or thirty years. Even with Chuck in my life, and Linda, there was a void.

I couldn't put my finger on it, but I knew my life was not moving forward. I knew I couldn't change the facts. I thought it was all Susan.

I must tell you her story someday.

I think what was happening to me was the memory of you coming to the surface, even though I didn't know it. Believe me when I say (please don't be hurt) you were so buried in my mind, like dead, that I did not think about you, because I wouldn't allow myself to.

If you hadn't found me, I would not have been able to put it all together. I never could have put Susan to rest. Thank you.

How could I have buried so much love forty-five years ago? All the tears I shed. Staying two weeks at St. Elizabeth's after you were born and not going up one flight of stairs to see you.

Still, it's really true about a mother's love. Nothing is deeper. Here I am sixty-five and you're forty-five. You found me and even though I had never seen you before, this overwhelming thing is happening to me with such force that there's no stopping it.

Why? Is it because I'm your mother? Yes. It is because I am your mother that I can behave this way with you, almost a stranger.

If you were a fraud, I would know it. This is powerful stuff we're dealing with here.

My feelings are so deep, so profound—the same as when Susan died—only this is like a birth and the joy I feel is inconceivable. One minute I'm fearful and the next I'm in Heaven. Eventually you will know me well enough to realize that I'm not trying to make you into Susan, or replacing her.

100

Just as our Linda has her own spot, you have your own very special spot, only I was totally unaware that it was there and waiting for you all these years. And to think, you might not have found me, to give me this gift.

Yesterday, I simply loved talking to you. Your voice, everything about our conversation was so much fun, music to my ears. Mike, did you ever in your life expect to have such an avalanche of emotions blasted at you?

Don't worry, it will be okay. I'll settle down and be normal, whatever normal is. Having no history of our own, there is no record of conflict between us; therefore, we can really communicate.

Maybe I'm taking a big chance writing all this, but so far I think you can take it. You wanted to know me and I feel I can do this, because I wouldn't open up if I didn't feel you are somewhat like me. I've never done this before.

Why you? A stranger, really, who is not a stranger. It's there, at the core and it's getting bigger and bigger. Already, in one short week, you have improved my life. Thank you. I'm finding real peace, something I had been searching for since Susan died and I think even before.

Peace.

I hope it will last; I think it will. I remember saying how hard it was, trying to find the pieces of my life so I could put myself back together again. But one piece wasn't there.

Now I can see that you were that missing piece, and I can move on, thanks to your searching and finding me. I feel so wonderful and I can't wait to tell you.

Writing these letters does help, because after reading them I can understand what is happening to me. Linda was right. I'm falling in love with my own son. I never mailed the letters but I did read them to Mike over the phone.

With our wedding anniversary approaching on August 21, just ten days after receiving Mike's letter, the feeling of euphoria is very strong. Both Chuck and I are filled with excitement and joy. We decide to celebrate our anniversary by purchasing a special bracelet for me, to commemorate this blessed event, as if we had just had a child.

Looking at the bracelets with the salesman, we both must have a glow about us, because he seems to notice. Bursting to tell someone, we decide to tell him our story. He's very happy for us and keeps looking at me with a searching look, with a certain respect. I can feel it and I find it very interesting.

We go to our usual jeweler next, who knows us pretty well. He notices our happiness and as our story unfolds in bits and pieces, he beams and is delighted for us and I see the same look that everyone has when they hear of an adopted child and a birth-mother finding each other. I notice he's looking at me with the same searching look as the other salesman. I can feel it. Very strange.

I wonder, is it my age or because I look too respectable today to have had that kind of experience? Or is it the fact that I am willing to expose my past by talking about it? Regardless, it is respect that I see in their eyes.

Everywhere Chuck and I go, people keep looking at us. We look happy and our excitement is obvious. When I see myself as we pass the mirrors in the mall, I'm shocked to see a gray-haired, sixty-five-year-old me, instead of a young vital twenty-year-old, because I feel so young again.

It's all very bewildering and wonderful. Something unique is happening to me. Chuck and I are having a great time and life is very exciting.

14

LOOKING BACK

L ooking back, I realize that there are stages involved in the reunion process of building a relationship. The emotions for both of us are new and unfamiliar.

The craving to know everything about each other. The yearning to be together. The uncomfortable feeling of awkwardness and the embarrassment of everyone watching us. The feelings involved were totally consuming. After many long phone discussions with my son about his life and mine, we realized we were building a deep trust for each other.

During one of our early conversations, I remembered a *dream* I had about Susan a couple of weeks before I received Mike's letter. I told him I seldom remembered my dreams and hardly ever dreamed about Susan. But this dream woke me up with a jolt. I sat on the edge of my bed feeling very disturbed and wondering what it meant. I explained to Mike that in the dream I was in a house that was a combination of all the houses I had lived in.

The house was full of all my family members, including Aunt Beth and Uncle Harold, and I saw Susan and then couldn't find her. After searching the house I found her in one of the bedrooms lying on her side on a twin bed with her back to me. As I entered the room and looked over her body, she turned her head and pointed to a baby and smiled at me.

As I was telling Mike about the dream, I strongly felt that Susan had been sending me a message. "Mike," I told him, "she was showing me a baby. It was a child I had never seen before." We felt that, without our knowing it, some higher force was working to cause our reunion when it did. We both found it comforting to believe that it had been Susan.

During this period, while talking on the phone, I remembered I had made a tape recording on December 3, 1992, Mike's birthday, almost a year before he found me. I told him that I was struggling at the time with depression. I knew I had a lot of anger, so I decided to tape-record my feelings and release some of my pent-up rage.

I remembered that I might have whispered at the end of the tape, "Happy birthday, John." I vaguely recall being astonished at letting that slip out. I told Mike that if I had said those words, it was the first time since he had been born that I had ever recorded his name or, for that matter, ever said his name.

After hanging up I searched until I found the tape. I played it and as I listened to my voice I realized how different my life had been at that time. Then there it was, at the very end of the tape: "Happy birthday, John."

I immediately called Mike and told him. We agreed that strange, unexplainable things had been happening to me while he was searching for me. Some powerful force was at work.

Eight months before Mike found me, in January of 1993, I had been in a very depressed state of mind, feeling I was not moving forward with my life. I absolutely could not find any peace.

I finally decided I needed counseling. I told the counselor I felt that my state of mind related to Susan and that I needed to start writing my book about her in order to heal. The counselor agreed. Then she told me about a friend of hers who had just written a book, and maybe it would help me. Would I like to read it? She handed me a copy and told me the author was a birth-mother. It was the first time I heard that term.

I amazed myself as I told her that I too was a birth-mother, because it was not my practice to mention that fact to anyone.

I read the book to see if it would help me to get started writing my book about Susan. I was very moved by the birth-mother's story and the long search she endured before she found her daughter. However, I didn't relate to the story because it was so different from mine.

After reading the book I realized for the first time that I hadn't had just one loss in my life, but two. I had a baby, a boy, and I gave him away. That was a loss, a major loss, but I didn't remember grieving. I wondered why. I started thinking about it and was astounded that until then I had never considered it a loss to give up my child for adoption. For several months I couldn't get over the fact that I had two losses.

Since my reunion with my son, and remembering these other experiences, I realize how deeply I was in denial since his birth. Even after reading the book by the birth-mother, I continued to stuff and bury my past in order to stay in denial.

In May, 1993, as our reunion was getting closer, my memory of Mike nee John broke through when my daughter Linda's friend was found by her daughter. I told them my story so freely, so matter-of-factly. To me, it was just a story I was telling. I wouldn't allow myself to even feel that it could have happened to me. Denial.

When I told Chuck about Linda's friend and what a great event her reunion was for her, he said, "Beth, if you ever want to search for your son, I would be happy to help you."

"Chuck, that is so thoughtful of you," I said. "Thank you, but I could never do that. I just couldn't ever do that. It will never happen."

I was very touched by Chuck's offer, but searching for my son or his looking for me was just unthinkable. I felt I had no right.

When I received Mike's letter on August 11, 1993, just a few months after these events, *I was totally stunned!*

Learning about my son and about myself at the same time, I knew I needed to understand more about adoption and adoptees. I read many books and learned some very disturbing things. I was beginning to feel terrible as I started to learn about adoption and adoptees.

Knowing Mike had been at St. Elizabeth's Home for Unwed Mothers for the first four months of his life made me furious with myself. Learning that the first four months are the most important of a child's life caused me great pain to realize I had let that happen. To this day I don't know why he was there so long.

Being naive, I just assumed the nuns at St. Elizabeth's were arranging the adoption and were taking care of everything. What I felt now was guilt, pure and simple guilt, for not knowing what I had done to my child.

After reading another book with a happy ending, written by a man who was Mike's age about his search for his mother, I recognized that I owed Mike an apology. I hadn't realized how insensitive I was to ask Mike during our very first phone conservation, "Why would you want to search for me?" I thought Mike should feel angry at me because I had given him away. After reading the book, I understood that Mike must have wondered all his life about his background and his biologocal mother and father.

I never thought about how deep those feelings would be. Now I understood his need to know more about himself. I was sorry I had asked him, "Why?" I could see the reason he was so intense in his search, and I hoped he would forgive me.

I can only compare my ignorance to people who said really dumb things to me when Susan was dying. I was appalled when—on two different occasions, just days after Susan died—people asked me if I would search for my son now. I couldn't believe they would think I could just go pluck him out of thin air to replace Susan. No one could replace her, ever. If I searched for Mike and found him, I believed he would always think I was trying to replace Susan, so it was all the more reason for me not to search.

I felt I had no right to look for him then. I thought it was terrible of those people to have asked such a question of me after Susan died, but they didn't know better, just as I didn't know what it had been like for Mike. It was the first part of my education about the world of adoption.

By the end of September, six weeks after my reunion with Mike, Chuck and I had visited Mike and his wife Linda four times. Each visit was very awkward. Although it was thrilling to see him, it was almost painful trying to be nonchalant about it. There were always other people around. We knew that everyone was happy for us, but we both agreed that they expected us to act as though we had known each other since his birth—an impossibility.

This new man in my life just happened to be my son. All I wanted to do was stare at him, and I couldn't because people would not take their eyes off us. I wanted to ask him a million questions. I wanted to hold his hand and put my arm around him, but it wouldn't look right.

I wanted to tell him why I had given him up, but I didn't want to tell him in front of other people, not even family members. It was just too personal, too private.

After our last visit, I knew I couldn't go through that again. I could not continue pretending to be a casual friend when I felt like a mother who had just discovered she had a child. I didn't know what to do. I couldn't even talk about it to my husband Chuck.

No one seemed to understand or even notice that we might need some time together alone. Thinking of the twenty-three Beth Kanes across the United States on Mike's search list, I wanted Mike to know I wasn't just a name on a list. I wanted an identity. I'm me, *this* Beth Kane, Mike's mother. I wanted him to know me and who I am. In order to do that I needed to have some time alone with him.

It became difficult for us to even talk on the phone in front of others. I finally worked up the courage and wrote Mike a letter telling him that I couldn't act like a nonchalant, casual friend any longer. We needed time alone. I was a nervous wreck for days, thinking I had really blown it and it would be the end of our relationship.

When his letter arrived, to my relief he said he was looking forward to spending a day with Chuck and me and even had a date chosen, October 6, 1993. And so began the next stage of our relationship.

15

ONE HOUR ALONE

As I anxiously waited for the day of Mike's visit to arrive, my emotions fluctuated between euphoria and fear. I was afraid of doing something wrong and then he would disappear. After not knowing him for forty-five years, I would be devastated if I lost him now. I had to do this right, be myself and let him get to know me.

I already knew that I loved him.

I wished I had something to give him. Something from the past, something to connect him with the time he was born. But I didn't have anything from that time. Naturally, I wouldn't have kept anything from Henry. Then I remembered.

While working at the Federal Reserve Bank in 1947, I had been a member of the women's basketball team. The bank and other big companies in San Francisco had sponsored the Women's Industrial League.

It was fun. I was able to leave work early to practice in Chinatown. Our team was good and we came in second place at the end of the season. I had been engaged to Henry when the season started, but he had broken our engagement by the time it ended.

A celebration had been planned for all the teams in the league to receive their awards at the Palace Hotel on Market Street. No longer engaged to Henry, I didn't have an escort. I don't know how I found the courage to ask Henry to escort me anyway, but he knew of the event and politely accepted. This was before he had announced his engagement to someone else.

It was an elegant affair, and I received a medal, as did everyone else on our team. The bank got a trophy, and it was still on display in the 1970s, when Susan worked there.

I was very thankful that I had something to give Mike, something I received the night that Henry and I were together and I was pregnant, even though we did not know it at the time. The medal was about one inch long and just for fun I would occasionally wear it on a chain around my neck, never letting anyone forget that I had won a sports medal.

I debated with myself over and over again. Should I give it to Mike? Is it right? I decided it was, and that it really belonged to him. So once again, by the time he arrived at my front door, I was trembling and out of breath. I asked Chuck if he could leave the house for an hour so Mike and I could be alone. Chuck was as anxious to spend time with Mike as I was, feeling he had a stepson that he wanted to get to know better, but he reluctantly agreed to do as I asked.

Mike and I were each self-conscious being alone and didn't know how to behave at first. Then we started looking at pictures from his childhood and growing up years. Soon we were enjoying ourselves as we looked at mementos from each other's lives. It seemed so strange, looking at a little boy who was my child and not knowing him.

It was comforting, though, seeing how happy his childhood had been. He was happy to see pictures of Susan and Linda as little girls and throughout their adolescence. We exchanged several pictures and I even found pictures of myself taken before I married Chuck. I wanted Mike to know what I looked like as a young woman and Mike wanted me to have a picture of him as a young man who still had hair. In one picture when he was seventeen he looked very much like me.

While showing me the pictures, Mike told me of his childhood and his schooling. He enjoyed his growing up years and his parents taught him to be a good citizen, well-mannered and polite. He had a good education, and I was happy to learn of his early life. Mike loves and respects his parents and appreciates the high standards they had for him.

I joked, "Wait a minute. You mean you didn't have a chauffeur driving you to school every day?"

I told Mike how I had always thought he was with a rich family and everything was supposed to be "peaches and cream." We laughed. I explained that I could understand now why I had made myself think he was with a wealthy family.

I told him as much as I could about his father. I wanted him to know that his father was not a bad person, because he wasn't. I tried to piece together the rumors and story about Henry for Mike. He was very interested and said that after knowing me, he knew his father couldn't have been a bad person. I took that as a compliment.

Suddenly I said, "Mike, I've been trying to think of something I could give you, something that connects you with everything that happened way back then. It seems so corny and small, but I think I found something."

"Please," he said. "You don't have to give me anything. I found you and that's enough."

"No, wait, I'll go get it."

I ran upstairs and found the medal, then wrapped it in a tissue.

"Here it is," I said, coming back down the stairs and sitting on the couch next to Mike. "This is such a small thing."

I felt awkward and embarrassed as I took his hand in mine and placed the tissue-wrapped gift in it. I told him the story of the medal, and the night I received it.

"So you see, Mike, we were all together on May 15, 1947—you, your father and me."

I opened the tissue in his hand.

"It's the medal I won, engraved with my name and the date. It's yours, Mike. You should have it. I want you to have it."

I closed his hand around it and looked at him with tears in my eyes, and saw that his eyes were full of tears too. He held it for a long time, then looked at me and with a choked voice said, "Thanks, Mom. I'll cherish it forever. It means a lot and I'll keep it with your picture that I always have with me. Thank you."

I felt very close to him and there was a deep respect for each other. A deep sense of love was present as well. We talked about the events surrounding his birth. I was able to explain some of my reasons for deciding to give him up. But I also told him I was having a hard time now understanding how I could have done that. Mike told me that he didn't remember ever feeling angry at me for giving him up. He always felt that I must have had a good reason.

After receiving the file from the attorney and reading the letters, Mike understood more of the story. I wanted to tell him even more. But one hour alone wasn't enough time. Still I had a chance to really connect some events of the past to the present for Mike. I could feel that our time together had been beneficial for him too.

Chuck returned, and seeing these two special men in my life together was a joy to me. They had so much in common and were very comfortable and relaxed with each other. Chuck has high standards, so when I saw that he very much approved of Mike, I was delighted.

Chuck told me again how much Mike reminded him of my brother, Bill, who always seemed as if he were Chuck's older brother and always appreciated Chuck's success in his career in law enforcement, and the Marines. Mike wanted to know more about Susan, so we showed him a video of her thirty-fifth birthday party. Bill and Sue were visiting from South Carolina at that time, so Mike would be able to see more of the family.

On this video Susan was talking to the camera, sending a message to her cousins that Bill and Sue would take home with them. The video Mike saw of Susan that day had been filmed less than two weeks before Susan became bedridden, but you would never know it.

She was smiling and joking and having fun for the camera. The video of Susan is not sad, and when I watch it today, it makes me smile to remember her great personality and spirit. Mike was pleased and proud to know how courageous his sister had been. I needed him to know about Susan and what she was like. I thought it would also help him to understand me.

Mike spent the whole day with us at our home and it was a very happy day for me. I had needed to spend time alone with my son, and we'd had one wonderful hour.

After our day together Mike felt it would be nice to write about his life in story form for me to have. He wrote of his childhood adventures, his career in law enforcement, about being a writer, and being a father to two wonderful girls.

I really appreciated his thoughtfulness, but reading about my son being raised by someone else had a disquieting effect on me. Still, I was eager to know everything about him—about all the years I had missed. We both felt that we were creating a relationship built on fun and laughter and the joy of discovery. Having the same sense of humor was wonderful. We became best friends, more than best friends.

We decided to always be truthful with each other, no matter what—to never let anything build up between us that would cause either of us not to understand the other. We loved each other as mother and son.

16

SEVENTH HEAVEN

As our first Holiday Season approached, we had some sorting out to do. We were a new extended family, but not really. So we became a "day-after" family. We spent the day after Thanksgiving at Mike and Linda's home, and Mike and Linda and their two daughters came to our home the day after Christmas. It worked out well.

Even after having spent our one hour alone together, each time we saw each other there were other people around. We agreed it was like seeing each other for the first time again—trying to decide what to wear, how to behave. We weren't able to talk to each other much. I became self-conscious again and felt like an idiot.

The only time I could be myself with him was on the phone. We discussed how strange it feels to have everyone act as though Mike has known me his whole life. We decided that a person who was not an adoptee or a birth-mother in reunion would never really understand.

I worried that Mike would think he had a fruitcake mother—the term I used was flibbertigibbet—a silly, flighty person.

Spending the day after Thanksgiving at Mike and Linda's was wonderful. Their home was warm and inviting, and they were active and successful. All the little things of a family's daily life were there, but I had no part in it. The feeling I had being there was unreal.

He was my son, yet I knew very little about his present life. I compared the feeling to how differently I felt visiting our daughter's home where I felt a part of it. I was sad for all the lost years without Mike. But at the same time, I felt grateful to be there and to be starting this new relationship with my son and his wife.

We went with them to the County Fairgrounds for a Christmas Crafts show. As we walked along the Fairground paths and met the local people, it was obvious that Mike and Linda were well known. Mike was on the board of some organization or other and seemed to take an active role in everything that went on there.

Many of their friends knew of Mike's long search for his mother and were very happy for him. Introducing me with a big sweep of his arm extended toward me, he beamed as he said, "And this is my mother!" I felt like a movie star.

His friends circled around us, staring with curiosity. Reunions like ours seem to make everyone happy. These people had known Mike for years and saw his excitement when he introduced me. I felt giddy with happiness. When Linda introduced Chuck as Mike's stepfather, Chuck was delighted. It was a great day and we all enjoyed each other. We were building a history.

In a new wonderful dreamworld, preparing for the "day after" Christmas at our home, I remember how different I felt trimming this Christmas tree compared to many of the recent years. The sadness was gone, and in its place was something I couldn't describe. I only remember the exhilarating joy I felt.

Our home has mementos from our travels and each has a story. Our furniture, acquired over the years, is a mixture of styles that surprisingly look good together. We like our home. I have achieved the goals I dreamed about when I was a small child in San Francisco, because it all came together the day after Christmas that year.

Trying to plan a Christmas dinner threw me for a loop. There would be too many people for a sit-down dinner, so I had to serve buffet-style. Our new family is Mike and his wife, Linda, their daughters Kim and Seana, and Seana's husband, Glen, along with our son-in-law, Tom, Susan's husband, and their children Stephanie and Greg.

And, of course, my right arm, my daughter Linda and her daughter Guinevere plus Chuck and myself.

Knowing how I behave when Mike is around, I was having a terrible time. I would be meeting Seana and Glen for the first time. And Stephanie and Greg would meet their new uncle and cousins. I feared I would never be able to get dinner on the table. I was desperate.

Once again, Linda saved the day with a brilliant idea. I was appalled by it, for this was a momentous occasion, with the whole family together for the first time. Dinner should be better than anything I had ever done. I've served many fine dinners over the years, and *no way* was I going to serve Kentucky Fried Chicken for Christmas dinner. No way!

Well, that's what we had and it was a great success. Greg and Stephanie, who have had all their Christmas dinners at our home, were surprised, but pleased.

Everyone had said, "Don't go to any trouble." I didn't, and everyone loved the food. I was beginning to wonder if Mike might think we always had take-out food or cold-cuts.

"I do cook, you know," I told Mike and his wife, "so you have to come back for a real home-cooked meal soon."

We had a wonderful time. Of course, it was awkward, but after all, it was our first holiday together. I was thrilled to meet Seana, a beautiful young woman who thought I was "neat." Glen was enjoying himself watching his wife's new extended family. Seana looked the same size as Kim and at the end of the evening, when I hugged each of them I had the same familiar feeling. I had no doubt that they each were a part of me. Mike and I knew all our loved ones were thrilled and happy and we felt "on stage."

Linda said, "Mom, you're always talking about writing a book. Why don't you and Mike write a book together? It's a great story."

Stephanie and Greg were taking everything in, fascinated. Their father, Tom, was happy for me and for his children. He thought Mike and his family were good people and he was thrilled when he noticed Kim's resemblance to Susan. Soon after receiving Mike's Special Delivery letter, I was having a struggle telling Stephanie and Greg about their grandmother's having had a child when she was not married.

I asked Stephanie, "How will I tell Gregory?" I was concerned about how he would feel about me.

"Nana," Stephanie immediately replied, "Greg is fourteen and going into high school. And Nana, this *is* the '90s."

"Well, Stephanie, you know, I'm still somewhat in the '40s. Thanks for being encouraging."

But I still didn't have the courage to tell Greg, so Stephanie told him for me. They were both very happy to have an Uncle Mike, their mother's brother.

So, as our first post-reunion Holiday Season drew to a close, both of our families had met each other. Everyone seemed delighted with this new wonderful feeling of being reunited. As for me, I was in Seventh Heaven.

17

PAIN AND GUILT

By February 1994, I had known Mike for more than six months. We were either faxing each other letters or talking on the phone, so our communication was up and running. During the same time, I had been reading every book I could find about the biological and emotional impact of the reunion on a mother and her child.

I needed to find something to relate to, something to explain the emotional upheaval I was experiencing. I decided, after reading the "Adoption Triangle" about birth-mothers, adoptive parents and adoptees, that if I wanted to keep this relationship going, I had a lot of work to do. One of the first things I learned was how fortunate I was to have a good relationship with my son. I cried while reading.

I knew that I still needed to grieve the long-ago loss of baby John (now Mike) and what I had missed when I walked away from him. I agonized for months.

Mike had done the searching for me, so I felt that he should set the pace of our relationship. For weeks I had the feeling of being a brand new mother. But deprived. Again.

It wasn't fair, I thought, that I never got to hold him in

my arms as a baby, and that's what I wanted to do. It made me very angry that I wasn't able to do that. Who was I to blame? No one but myself. I had made the decision then and today I still believe it was the right decision.

Knowing that, however, did not stop the terrible feeling of being deprived that had stayed with me for some time. Whenever I wanted, I still could not see or touch or talk to my child (who irrationally seemed like a baby to me.) I was overwhelmed with such a strong sense of yearning that it was like sitting on my bed at St. Elizabeth's again, knowing he was up there in the nursery and not being able to go up to the nursery to see him. The yearning and searching for satisfaction increased every day.

Finally one day, I recognized that this yearning was a major grieving symptom similar to what I had experienced after Susan died. Then I knew that I would not find what I was looking for, because the only satisfaction for me would be that Mike belonged to me, and *that* could never be. I had given him to someone else.

It was devastating to realize this, but I could not go back and undo what I had done. I had to face the facts. I told myself, "He is a grown man, not a baby. He is not mine, never was and never will be." It was a hard thing to accept.

Then I realized that if I had even seen a finger or a toe of his after he was born, I could have been like this, with this overwhelming yearning, for my entire life, and it could have ruined my life. But my life had *not* been ruined. Thank God, I had listened to the nuns and had not taken those steps up the one flight, just to have a peek, just one peek at my baby. Now I remember thinking about doing that.

How could I have blanked out so much heartache?

I knew that I had to snap out of all this. It was not an easy time for me. Reading the few books describing what other birth-mothers went through helped. The love I felt for my son was overwhelming. I could not stop thinking about him. I thought it wasn't right to feel this way. I was going overboard.

Then, while reading the case studies and learning that most birth-mothers feel the same overwhelming love, I felt better. But reading did not help me to understand why I felt this overwhelming love. I didn't remember feeling this way when my girls were born. This was all probably natural under the circumstances.

When you have a child in *normal* circumstances and you are going to take that child home with you from the hospital to love and raise, your love for that child is immediate. Every day your love grows and grows until it becomes a part of you and your life. Slowly you form a bond, that is so deep, with a mother's love for her child that the child becomes your life. I did not give to my son in normal circumstances.

One day during this period, while on my knees planting flowers in our garden, I was listening to a tape given to me by a birth-mother friend. The tape had been recorded at a conference of the American Adoption Congress (AAC), headquartered in Washington, D.C. The speaker, a psychologist was an adoptee and an adoptive parent. She knew what she was talking about.

Wearing a headset, listening intently, with my hands in the dirt, I heard her describe how a child, even at birth, knows when he is abandoned. Being so familiar with the mother's womb and not finding that familiar person after birth, the child feels an immense feeling of sadness and yearning.

I stopped planting and started crying. It was hard to accept all this, but I understood it immediately. I felt horrible, remembering that Mike was not adopted until he was four months old. I realized what a terrible thing I had done to him. I put my face in my dirty, gloved-hands and sobbed. Sobbed with deep convulsive painful sobs. I couldn't stop. I wanted to call Mike right then, to beg his forgiveness, but I was too afraid.

The speaker went on to say a few things about birth-mothers. I sat there, my legs aching, listening, scarcely believing it. My feelings were the same as those she described on the tape.

My body was screaming out for that baby, at that moment, forty-five years after he was born. Although I was upset, it helped to hear someone describe what I was feeling. I didn't remember having such feelings when Mike was born because I had stuffed and buried all the natural feelings I had then.

The birth-mother carries and loves the child in her womb and grows as attached as is humanly possible. She delivers her baby and then walks away without seeing or holding the child—ripping apart the most natural bond in the world: mother and child.

Now I understood why I felt this overwhelming love. What I had done was the most unnatural thing on earth. No wonder I had been in so much pain as I sat there for two weeks and looked up at the nursery window.

I thought *How am I going to live with this? I have to find a way, because the miracle of our being reunited is so glorious.*

I listened intently to the speaker as she spoke to all birth-mothers in the audience. I could visualize her pointing her finger at me as she said, "You birth-mothers, listen. If you have not grieved the fact that you gave up a child for adoption and had this great loss, you better do it now." She made it very clear. "Go get in bed, get in a fetal position and start."

The terrible feeling stayed with me for days. I knew what I had to do, but I didn't know how. My fear of something happening, of losing my son again, was so overwhelming that one day during this period I panicked and called him. I needed to hear from Mike that he was still there, and that he still felt the same about me. I cried and apologized for behaving this way. I had a sick fear that he would not understand—but, thank God he did.

He told me that he kept forgetting he was way ahead of

me, because he had done the searching and felt secure in our relationship from the beginning. He understood that for me it was very different and it would take me longer to gain the confidence that he will never change his mind about me.

With all this in my mind and still reading all the books I could find, I decided to write to the authors, stating that I did not find *me* anywhere in all the case studies. I really needed help that would explain my anguish in order to understand more completely.

I wrote that I considered myself an expert on grief. Why was it, I wrote, that after Susan died, the loss of Mike did not surface? I knew that I did not grieve the loss of him, and I was having a very difficult time understanding why. Two authors responded.

Merry Block Jones author of *Birthmothers*, which covers the case studies of more than seventy women who relinquished their babies for adoption wrote:

> Dear Ms. Kane:
> I was moved by your letter. It sounds like you've had your share of coping to do, and I encourage your efforts to seek support in what you called "the long path" of healing.
> What you are going through, at long last, is normal and healthy. *Not* to feel grief was probably your best survival tool at the time of your surrender and for years afterwards.
> But now, you sound as if you're bursting with pent up, long-buried feelings. And, although it's scary, difficult and painful, you need to do it if you're going to put all your emotional pieces back together into an integrated, self-acknowledged whole.
> You are not alone. Good luck.

Both authors who responded told me that under the circumstances I did the only thing I could have done for survival. When Mike was born, I buried all my grief. The loss of

Mike hadn't surfaced when Susan died because I couldn't have handled the pain at that time either.

They both explained that a person can only endure so much pain at one time, and I guess that's what happened to me. They also told me that I needed to grieve the loss of my baby John, who became Mike, so I could move on. They thought I was a strong person, but I did not feel strong. I knew, however, that I had to do as they suggested.

When you have a child and walk away as I did, you are forced to bury all the love you have when you are carrying that child, especially when you turn yourself off and take the advice of everyone else. That was exactly what I had done.

After a reunion with your child, it doesn't take long for all that deep mother and child love to surface. When the biological emotions hit, the impact is overpowering. You feel out of control. You have no idea what's happening. It feels wonderful and frightening at the same time.

Having forty-five years of buried love surface all at once was an emotional Big Bang. At the time, I had no explanation for any of it because it was an emotion I had never felt before. After all, the child I gave away had come back, and now I just could not get enough of him. Nonetheless, I did not feel secure and had a great fear of losing him again.

At this point, when I realized just how much of my son's life I had missed, I felt extremely sorry for myself. I raged about my life. I've always been deprived, starting with when I was a little girl, and knowing my father didn't like me. My mother was always too busy dealing with her problems. We were poor, I had a lousy education—it was easy to be angry, to feel sorry for myself.

Some man took advantage of me, and I had given my son away without ever seeing him. My wonderful daughter had died. *Damn! Why her?* I raged and raged with anger and self-pity. I felt I had plenty of reason. Life wasn't fair.

But on the other hand, out of my mother's six children, only two of us had made successful lives, Bill and I. I should be thankful that I had been given the opportunity to be with my aunt Beth and uncle Harold, to know what a normal life could be like. I was able to set and fulfill my goals. I met and married Chuck and had given birth to Susan and Linda. I have wonderful grandchildren, and now two more. Mike is now in my life. *How can I feel sorry for myself?* The love and support I have from my family is always with me.

I had reached the depths of my sorrow when the barrier around my soul cracked and I faced my guilt.

> That day in the garden while on my knees,
> the tears flowed freely and my healing began,
> as I accepted my guilt and let myself grieve.

How fortunate for me that Mike had the perseverance to search long enough to find me and give me this wonderful gift. I am so grateful.

18

MY FAIRY TALE

Chuck was the first to notice a difference in me soon after Mike and I were reunited. He mentioned that a big part of me had been missing for years; he had known it, but hadn't known why. Our relationship improved from the first day of Mike's appearance.

One day Chuck and I went through all our early albums, trying to find pictures of me as a young woman to give Mike so he would know what his mother looked like back in those days. While looking, Chuck and I read our old letters to each other. He had been in the Marines when I first met him and he was not discharged until several months after we were married. As we reread the letters, it was as if we were falling in love all over again. My appreciation for Chuck and his for me was renewed.

I remember when I first met Chuck. My sister and I went to pick up his sister at their home. The three of us were going to a dance hall called the German House in Oakland. I remember that Chuck was sitting in a chair in his living room and it seemed as if his long legs took up the whole room. It was the last night of his leave from the Marines and after calling his friends, he found that he did not have a date.

I had been off work for a month because of a ruptured appendix, and with the doctor's permission this was my first night out. I thought Chuck was good-looking and soon after we arrived at the German House, I was thrilled when he joined us.

Chuck and I ended up spending the whole evening together, but the next day he left for Hawaii and would be gone for two weeks. I was happy when he called me before his ship pulled out, and after talking for some time he finally said, I'll write you, will you answer?" "Yes" I said.

When I received his first letter, he asked me for a date. It took hours to compose my letter accepting the date. He returned and asked me to marry him—one month after our first date. I guess Aunt Beth had been right, because Prince Charming came along and gave me an engagement ring.

The day after I received it, I bought twelve place-settings of sterling silver flatware that took months to pay for. After the expense of our beautiful wedding five months later, I carried the silverware home on the bus because we didn't have a car. In fact, the $400.00 worth of silverware was three times more expensive than our first car, purchased a month after the silverware was paid for. I look back now with a smile, realizing how my priorities were rather backwards. But I had started working on my goals for building my fairy tale world.

Chuck and I were a good-looking couple—everyone said so. He was tall and slender and perfectly proportioned, big shoulders, long arms, long legs and big feet. He was extremely handsome with dark brown wavy hair and steel blue-gray eyes.

I had been very flattered that he was taken by me. I was a tall and slender brunette with hazel blue-green eyes. Even though I was tall for a woman, I was still a foot shorter than Chuck. I loved his height and size and was so proud of him as we walked down the aisle.

We were married on August 21, 1949, and I wore my beautiful white wedding gown which society would have frowned on had it known of my past. Standing at the altar and getting married I still had this secret, but in my heart I knew that I was a good person. Aunt Beth told me that as I started down the aisle, she had been on her hands and knees crawling behind me, trying to straighten out my train.

My biggest thrill and honor, though, was that Uncle Harold gave me away. This cherished man was my uncle by marriage to Aunt Beth, my mother's sister. As I turned around after the ceremony and looked at Uncle Harold, I saw tears running down his cheeks. I wish he were alive today to know that my son has found me.

I remember so many things about Aunt Beth who was like a second mother to me. She was forever trying to improve me. "Bethie," she would say, "Stand up straight with your shoulders back and hold your head up. Don't look at your feet so much."

She wanted me to know how to act like a lady and dress like a lady. She would tell me, "If you have to cross your legs when you sit, Bethie, remember to pull your skirt down, never show your whole knee, just a hint. And always remember to have your "mad money" with you when you are on a date. You never know, you might need the money for a phone call or streetcar fare to get home."

Aunt Beth was a good influence on me and was very happy to watch me standing up straight as I walked down the aisle with Chuck. Four months after we were married, we put $100.00 down on our first home. Another goal achieved.

Susan was born a week after our first anniversary, and Linda, thirteen months to the day after Susan. So we had our own home and two daughters by the end of 1951. I had gone to work when Susan was four months old and then found out I was pregnant again and had to quit my job. When Linda was three months old, I went back to work again. I felt that as long as I was capable of earning money, I should.

Chuck was struggling to start his career in law enforcement, and I was trying to achieve a better life for our girls. Looking back, I can see now that I was trying to add to my fairy tale world. I remember always being intense as I worked hard to provide for our girls.

I had to prove to myself that I gave up a child for adoption because if I had kept him as an unwed mother, I would not have been able to provide the kind of life for him that I was determined to provide for Susan and Linda. I wasn't aware of this at the time, but now I understand why I had such a strong determination to succeed.

There were quite a few times during the years that my secret about having had a son and giving him up for adoption came to the surface—things I had completely forgotten. I remembered that after Linda was born and we had two daughters, a fleeting thought went through my mind. A punishment of some kind, no son for Chuck? *I had my chance*, I told myself. *I had a son and I gave him away.*

The thought occurred several times over the early years. All men want sons, and I felt that I had cheated Chuck somehow. There was no way we could afford more than our two children.

Another memory from around 1954: Soon after moving to our second home, the local Catholic priest came to our home and urged us to attend church. Father O'Neill sat in my living room, while Chuck slept because he was a police officer working the midnight shift, and Susan and Linda were in our back yard, still toddlers. Father O'Neill asked if we were turning our backs on our religion. I had the courage to be honest with him.

"We haven't gone to church because the Catholic Church believes that it's a sin to use birth control," I told him truthfully. "We cannot afford to have more that our two children."

"God will provide, if you have more children," Father O'Neill replied.

I sat there thinking, *He really believes that. What does he know about life?*

"God didn't provide when I was a child," I answered. "With six children in our family, we went to bed hungry many times. I feel it's more of a sin to bring children into this world if we are not able to provide them the kind of life they deserve."

I was surprised I had the nerve to say that.

His response to me was, "Don't you feel that you have enough love in your heart for more than two children?" The question was insulting. That man knew nothing of real life, and had no idea what was in my heart, or that I had already had a son that I had placed for adoption.

My secret came immediately to my mind. I wondered if he was right. *Was I being selfish? Didn't I have enough love in my heart?* Father O'Neill's cutting remark did not change my strong conviction not to have children that we could not provide a good life for. But it was a crushing remark that stayed with me for a long time.

Not too long after receiving Mike's Special Delivery letter, I called my niece, Sharon, and told her the good news. Of course, she had known for years. Her brother was the infant I was holding in the picture that Mike showed me the first night we met.

Sharon wrote to Mike soon after our reunion and welcomed him to the family. She told him that her mother remembered, when she had her baby twenty days after Mike was born, how I had cried looking at her son. I was surprised because I had no memory of that.

I do remember my mother telling me to be careful when I looked at my sister's baby. Now I remember the day my sister came home from the hospital. I don't know why, but she was at my mother's house and in my bed. I remember sitting on the chair in the corner, watching her and her baby, and feeling terrible.

I thought no one knew about me at that time and that I

was doing a good job of covering up. Now I can see that it was very obvious that I was a new mother too.

Sharon told me how much my daughter Susan had wanted to search for Mike. I remember Susan asking me many times as a teenager why I didn't look for him. Susan told Sharon she was going to look for him anyway, whether I liked it or not.

I remember being frightened by this thought: *What if Susan or Linda grew up and married their own brother?* When I signed the final adoption papers, the Social Worker covered the name of the adoptive parents, but the paper slipped and I saw a name. I always wondered if she did that on purpose.

When Susan kept talking about finding her brother, I called Chuck's sister, Dorothy, and told her my story for the first time. I wanted her to know the name I had seen on the adoption papers. I asked her to write it down, in case something happened to me and I died. What if Susan or Linda met and fell in love with a man with that name? I asked Dorothy to please make sure they didn't marry their brother.

I realize now how many times I had to keep the memory of Mike buried, but it kept popping up. So through the forty-five years of our separation, Mike came to the surface many more times than I had thought. I guess I had stuffed and buried all through the years and had added to what was already deep in my heart.

19

FINDING THE REST OF ME

It wasn't until after the first anniversary of the reunion with my son that I recognized the flashes I had been having at the beginning of our relationship, when everything had felt clean and pure. I felt so different. The secret I had hidden for so many years had caused me to deny a major part of myself and now that part of me was back.

The realization was sudden. I was surprised that it could have happened. By Mike's finding me he gave me back that part of me that had been buried deep in my heart with him, the Justine part. Why was it that I was just noticing now? Chuck had seen the difference in me, practically from day one.

I remember in the early stages of our reunion describing the feeling as "The other shoe has dropped." It had been hanging out there for forty-five years, waiting to be dropped, and I hadn't even known it.

The empty, melancholy feeling disappeared. I felt direction, and started living in the present with a sense of being whole that I couldn't remember having felt before. It was amazing to discover these feelings because I had always prided myself on knowing myself so well. I had to call Mike to tell him.

"Do you know what you did for me?" I asked. "You opened the door and gave me back myself. Thanks again for another gift."

His surprised reply was, "Wow, I'm glad."

Poor Mike. Every time I talked to him, I had some new revelation about something. He was a good listener, though. I'm happy he was patient with me as I worked my way through all the new things I was discovering about myself.

After a few more months of trying to sort things out, it became apparent that I needed to follow the advice of the experts in order to heal—to get to the serious business of remembering my life back in 1947 and to grieve the loss of my son.

One day I decided to call St. Elizabeth's. Discovering it was still there, I wondered if I should start there.

"I just called St. Elizabeth's," I told Chuck, "and it's still a home for unwed mothers. Can you believe that? After all these years. Maybe I should look at that building. What do you think? Would you mind driving to San Francisco, so I can see it with my own eyes?"

"Sure, if that's what you want to do. I'd be happy to."

Seeing the red brick building, with its big double doors made my heart pound. The building was indelibly impressed in my mind. Just by looking at the windows, I could still feel the power it held for me in 1947. It *had* happened. I *did* have a baby in that building.

I pointed out the chapel and the windows of the dining rooms and activity room to Chuck. I wanted to see my room and the nursery, but they faced the back of the building.

Chuck then took a picture of me by the gate. Standing there, looking at the stairs and double doors, it was as if time had stopped. Walking up those very same stairs when I entered, and remembering the day I had walked away from my child, I acknowledged it had happened and was surprised by how free I felt now that my secret was no longer a secret because my son had found me.

Seeing St. Elizabeth's after forty-six years took me back to another world—the world of 1947. The time when society encouraged me to have such a low opinion of myself, when secrets and shame were to be hidden at all cost—repressed and forgotten—buried deep in my heart.

Driving through downtown San Francisco on our way to the Bay Bridge, I remembered the San Francisco of 1947. A time of streetcars and trolleys, horns honking, the bells of cable cars clanging and the rush of automobiles on busy Market Street. A time of innocence and naiveté, still in the aftereffect of World War II. A time when the city was safe, when everyone on Market Street dressed up, and women wore hats and gloves and high heels. San Francisco was beautiful and exciting.

"Beth, how do you feel now after seeing St. Elizabeth's again?" Chuck asked as we drove home. "Do you think it helped you to remember more of the past?"

"Yes, it sure did. I remember how I felt. I remember the sadness. Just looking at the place carried me back to 1947. Thanks for bringing me over here, Chuck. You've been so great with everything that's happened since Mike found me."

"Hey," he responded, "I'm happy too. I like Mike, I think he's a great guy. But most of all, I see a difference in you. You're happy, and that's the way it should be."

While driving home I had time to remember even more. My lowest point was after Mike was born, going back home to the Housing Project and to my family. I was glad to know that the Project had been torn down. To this day I feel sorry for anyone who has to live in such a place.

I remembered being confronted by my brother Jack, my older sister and her husband after I had been home for a few months. They invited me out for drinks in a local bar. Sitting there, they informed me that they knew I'd had a son. They were sorry it had happened to me, but could not understand how I could have given up a child. They told me they thought I was selfish.

I felt surrounded and embarrassed. I had thought no one knew about my pregnancy or my son's birth. I didn't know what to say. I knew they would never understand how I had struggled with my decision to give my child the opportunity to have a decent life. My sister said that our stepfather Charlie had told our family friends about me and was asking to borrow money because, "Well, Beth's got herself in trouble." It made me feel sick with shame and humiliation.

"Oh!" the news took my breath away. I looked at my sister and asked, "Does mother know he's doing that?"

She replied in a sad voice, "I don't think so, Beth. Probably not."

I felt it was such a terrible betrayal. But it did help to convince me that if I had kept Mike and had tried to raise him in that environment, that kind of negative attitude would have been held by everyone. The baby and I would not have had a chance. The family didn't know how unselfish my decision had been.

As Chuck drove, I sat very quietly, remembering my childhood and how poor we were. Whenever we had a radio, I could listen to my favorite program, "I Love a Mystery." But eventually the radio would disappear. My stepfather would hock it, then take the money and gamble it away, trying to win enough money for food. I can remember a time when he came home with boxes of food after being out all night. We were all jumping around and excited, all except my mother, who was angry at him for gambling.

I remembered how I hated being poor. I hated wearing hand-me-down clothes to school and being embarrassed by all the kids knowing I was being given free milk. I hated moving once a year and going to nine different grammar schools, seven in Oakland and two in San Francisco.

The most embarrassing experience, however, was to have the lights and power turned off because my parents did not pay the bill. To have my friends see the flickering candles in our windows caused me the most humiliation because they would know the reason.

My childhood in Oakland with my mother and stepfather had been in such marked contrast to that part of my childhood spent in San Francisco living with my aunt and uncle. I could understand why I made my decision not to take Mike into the world of the Project. All of this history of my childhood had been fresh in my mind, I'm sure, when I was at St. Elizabeth's waiting for my child to be born and struggling to make my decision.

Having seen the finer things in life, I realized that living with my aunt Beth and uncle Harold was a wonderful life for me. I had the best of everything a child should have, I was not spoiled, and I appreciated everything. Maybe that was why they loved me so much and wanted to adopt me. I felt loved and was told continuously that I was a good girl. It's obvious to me that I certainly received all the love I needed in my childhood. I was very lucky.

All of these memories were very fresh in my mind when Chuck and I arrived home from San Francisco. It left me very depressed. After a few days of recalling and digesting the memories of my childhood years through the time of my son's birth, I started to feel better about my decision.

During the next few weeks, I rented old movies made in 1946 and 1947. Watching them, seeing the clothes, the cars and the innocence of life at that time, I was in the right frame of mind to start writing my story—for Mike and to answer the question of "Why?" for myself.

I remembered my alter ego Justine and what she had done. I sobbed and sobbed as I grieved all the circumstances surrounding my decision to give up my child. As I thought of Justine, I was relieved to remember and reassure myself that I did deeply love the child I was carrying. Being in denial for so many years, I found it difficult to believe that I couldn't remember. But now I felt again the deep pain and the terrible shame I had felt back then.

I remembered my anger and rage and felt it again for what I had done. I was convinced I did the right thing, and after some time I was able to forgive myself for giving up my son. It took me many days to work through my memories and my loss, until gradually I began to feel better. I looked at my son's baby pictures and finally *felt* the deep biological connection. I remembered talking to him and loving him before he was born.

I grieved over the loss of my son, John, (now Mike) just as I had grieved the loss of Susan. Only this time, I knew what was happening to me. And why it was happening. It was very painful, but once I faced what I had given up, and grieved that loss, I knew that I still had my child, my son. With my grief over Susan, the searing pain did not have a happy ending. Death is final.

After writing the story of myself as Justine and reading it several times, I knew I had to send it to Mike. I was anxious for him to know, at last, my whole story—his whole story—and hoped he would understand why I had made the decision to give him up for adoption.

A fax came to me from Mike a few days after he read the story. He was overwhelmed:

> Thank you for sharing your story with me. I was moved when I heard it, and even more so after reading it. I again felt that wave of emotion that poured over me each time I found a new piece of information about you during the search. It's been a while since having that feeling.
>
> To read of your life and emotions while I was a part of it is a little disconcerting, but not in a negative way. I don't mean that. What I mean is . . .
>
> I took that trip to Mississippi with you. I hung out in the hotels those terrible nights after returning to San Francisco with you.

I was there *too.*

Your story is as much a part of who and what I am as anything else in my life experience.

WOW!

That realization just hit me between the eyes and its residue is still with me as I write this. I'm sorry I was the cause of so much trauma and at the same time, I'm glad you did it your way. I've never felt particularly courageous, but I know now that courage runs through me in a life form directly from my MOTHER.

Seeing the video and hearing about such courage in my sister Susan, witnessing it in my youngest sister Linda, I now feel confident I'll have it should I ever need it.

Thank you.

I love you.

I cried with relief after reading Mike's letter. His deeply moving words touched me to the core of my being. I sent him a fax the same day:

Thank you! Thank you! You have made me happy for the rest of my life. Your words are so healing and soothing, just exactly what I needed from you, ACCEPTANCE of what I did!

Thank you from the bottom of my heart. I can't believe how lucky I am that you are the "You." I love you.

I wrote this poem and sent it to Mike along with the story.

THE WHY

My heart is in better shape today.
Why?

Because I cried and cried,
As I remembered the day you were born.

137

You are forty-six now,
You are my son,
And we've only just met.
Why?

Because we lost each other
When you were born.
I gave you to someone else.

That's what I remembered:
The Why.

I put myself back to that time,
And asked myself again and again,
Why couldn't you do it?

Because I remembered everything,
And how it really was.

I thought I was doing the right thing,
And today, I know I did.

You decided to search for me,
And you didn't give up.

Now that I know you,
I'm convinced
You are better off,
And it was right.

You are fine, strapping, handsome and tall.
I knew you would be.

I hope you think that what you found
Is sound.
I loved you then, as I do now.

I remembered the pain of my decision,
The pain of the sorrow,
And the pain of my broken heart.

But, my heart is in better shape today.
Why?

Because it was meant to be.
We are together again.

20

BEING THERE IN PEACE AND JOY

For the next few weeks I described my feeling as "Floating around on cloud nine, on my way to Seventh Heaven." Euphoria was back.

I found peace, knowing my son and having the confidence that he would always be there. It's hard to describe the difference in my life. A feeling of having both feet firmly planted on the ground. A new excitement for life.

A clearer vision. Happiness. Hoping I have enough time left to do all the things I want to do. Knowing I will know my son for the rest of my life.

Mike told me what a difference his finding me and his family background made in his life. He summed it up by saying, "I just know that you will always be there. Thanks for waiting for me to find you."

The next time we talked by phone, I told him, "Mike, I have asked myself many times since you found me why didn't I keep you. If I had and we had gone to live in my mother's household in the Project, it would have been terrible."

Feeling sad, I continued, "There were seven people crowded in our apartment and my mother was already raising my brother Jack's son. I would have had to go to work and leave you and that would have meant that my mother would have had to take care of you too."

I stopped to catch my breath as I was pouring my heart out to Mike; he was listening very quietly.

"I saw so many terrible things there. You would have been called names. I heard it happen to other little kids like you. I'm sorry, though, that I couldn't have found another way."

With a lump in my throat, I said, "I probably wouldn't have married Chuck either. Then I wouldn't have had Susan and Linda. I did do the right thing, Mike I know it. But it still hurts."

Taking a deep breath for courage, I told him, "Mike, you have to know, this is hard for me to say, but what happened way back then *did not* ruin my life. I had a good life and now you have made it all the better."

Mike responded quietly, with deep sincerity,

"I'm glad it didn't ruin your life. You did the right thing under the circumstances. It's also important for me to tell you that your decision didn't ruin my life either. I had a good life too. We're both lucky."

Then I remembered that long ago Halloween night in the scary flop house.

"Mike, do you ever remember being frightened on Halloween night with goblins and ghosts? Since, as you say, you 'hung out with me,' you could have a real hang-up about Halloween."

We both laughed. Our relationship at that moment was at its peak of respect, trust, admiration and unconditional love.

Several months after our reunion, my cousin Harilyn visited us. As she stood looking at the pictures on the bulletin board that I keep in my kitchen, she noticed the remarkable resemblance of my daughter Susan to Mike's daughter Kim.

141

"This is like a miracle, Beth. What a blessing for you." Harilyn said.

Seeing photographs of Mike as a ten- and twelve- year-old, she asked, "Is this Mike? He looks like Henry, doesn't he?"

Although I find I can't remember much about Mike's father, Henry, or what he looked like, my cousin Harilyn did. I had completely forgotten that she knew him.

"You were only twelve years old, Harilyn. You mean you remember what he looked like?"

"Yes," she said, "I remember he was tall and I thought he was very handsome, big brown eyes and dark brown straight hair. He had a nice smile. I remember you had a photo of him."

Staring at her, not believing what she was saying, I could see that she was trying to remember.

"Yes, I was only twelve," she said, "but I remember the photo was an 8 x 10 glossy. Don't you remember that?"

Henry, through all these years, was still unreal to me, as if he had nothing to do with any of this.

"My God, Harilyn, I simply have no memory of that picture and I can't even visualize what he looked like. It's strange what I've totally blanked out. Come to think of it, Harilyn, you're the only person still alive who met Henry."

Later on, when I related this story to Mike, he found it interesting and was pleased to have another description of his father. I wished I could tell him more.

I recalled the first night I met Mike and Linda, sitting in the restaurant, and how I was shocked by everything in the file. Seeing the name of June, my roommate at St. Elizabeth's made me think that the chain of events was remarkable.

Because June and I wanted to stay in touch, we broke the rules and exchanged our real names and phone numbers. I called her for help after the call from St. Elizabeth's when my son was 3 months old and still not adopted. June led me to Philip Adams, who just happened to be the type of lawyer who keeps good records for forty-five years—how amazing.

Thank God that in August 1993, attorney Adams believed that adoptees should have the right to their birth records and simply handed the file to Mike.

With the information about me there, Mike found me five days later. No wonder Mike and Linda were so excited when we first met. After he had been searching for so many years, it was another miracle.

After Mike read my story about me as Justine, he asked if I had forgiven my mother. I told him yes. It wasn't until Mike came back into my life that I even remembered the scary Halloween night I spent in the flophouse alone and pregnant. The memory caused me many hours of being hurt and angry with her.

Then I remembered how life had been for her at that time. Not very good. She and my stepfather were on some kind of welfare at that time and if she hadn't been home on November 1, 1947, she would not have been there to get the welfare check before my stepfather got his hands on it.

Knowing my mother, I realized she would not have left me alone that Halloween night under any other circumstances. It must have also been hard for her to send me as a small child to my aunt Beth in San Francisco to get me away from my father.

There was good reason for me to forgive my mother and to admire her as well.

Most of my mother's life, until she was seventy-five, had been spent raising children and grandchildren. Then she moved alone to a senior citizens' complex. Within one year she was on the Board of Directors.

She worked for the City of Oakland, helping old people. She marched on Sacramento with other seniors, protesting something—she even made the eleven o'clock news. She saw Prince Charles at the City Hall, and said she was so close she could have touched him. She went to Hawaii by herself, to visit a grandson who was in the Army.

She was eighty when she started taking art lessons, and I have her paintings framed and hanging on my wall. She was an active member and officer of the World War I Widows Association and went to their conventions.

It was fun watching my mother enjoy her later years, and I often wondered what her life would have been like if she had married different men.

Yes, I have forgiven my mother.

She lived to be ninety-four, and she worked very, hard and did the best she could for all of us. She taught me it's better to be honest and to stand on my own two feet. I wish she were alive today to share in all this happiness.

Mike and I have discussed many times how lucky we are. What if I hadn't told Chuck that I had had a baby before we were married? Receiving Mike's Special Delivery letter and reading it aloud to Chuck could have been a disaster.

Mike took a big risk and has thanked me many times for being the kind of person who *had* told Chuck. Not knowing what to expect when he sent the letter and not knowing what my circumstances would be, he and his wife Linda were very relieved when they heard my voice on their answering machine.

Mike told me that he and Linda heard me laughing and saying, "That's my husband you hear, telling me what to say." They could hear Chuck's voice in the background. They could both hear the excitement in our voices.

Thinking of all the different types of people in the world, and discovering that Mike is a great guy is another big plus. I remember saying to him one day after I had known him for awhile, "Thank God you're not a jerk, or a religious fanatic. You could have been anything. I'm so glad you're you."

Mike responded with, "Hey, what about me? Think about what kind of a person I could have found. I'm so glad you're you too."

The one mystery I haven't been able to solve is the exact time Mike was born and how much he weighed, so one day as we talked, I decided to ask him.

"Mike, do you recall hearing the exact time that you were born and how much you actually weighed? I know you were born around three in the afternoon and you weighed about eight pounds."

I told him that at this time I was feeling like a brand new mother, needing to know the precise details of his birth.

"I don't ever remember hearing that." Mike said. "In fact, I don't remember ever thinking about it."

I thought it was a typical male response, then he said, "But, I wasn't wearing a watch at the time."

Surprised at visualizing that, my quick response was, "Gee, I'm sure glad that you weren't." Our sense of humor really meshed.

I told him new mothers feel it's important to know that particular information for some reason, and I was still in the new mother stage. The strangeness of a situation like this is beyond anything one can imagine.

When I sent the first draft of this book to Mike, of course he thought it was wonderful. A woman who edits Mike's newspaper read and corrected the book for me and sent a note: "What a way to get to know someone! It's interesting how you and Mike have similarities in your writing styles."

I was stunned by her saying that, and thrilled by her observation.

Some of the things I have discovered since our reunion astound me. I have always thought that children acquired their body gestures, speech inflections and mannerisms from the environment of their daily lives. I would not have thought Mike's mannerisms and body language would be so much like mine and my brother Bill's.

How about the thought process? I would have thought it too would be formed by the daily environment. After getting to know Mike but not spending a great deal of time with him—most of our communication has been in writing and talking on the phone—it has become apparent that we are very much alike.

During our early conversations, sometimes I felt I knew what he was going to say before he said it, as if I could read his mind. I had the feeling that he could almost read mine, too. Our phone conversations are always comfortable and easy-going. We can talk on any topic and never run out of things to say. His voice and thought processes are so familiar that it is like talking to myself. He emphasizes certain words as I do.

Even his favorite swear word is the same as mine. Having the same sense of humor, sometimes our phone conversations are one continuous stream of laughter and fun as we each build on what the other has said.

There are so many things we have talked about over the years, learning about each other. We had so many questions of the "How do you feel about that?" nature, and discovered our political thoughts and religious thoughts were the same.

I now think Mother Nature has a lot to do with this. Think of all the beautiful flowers in the world that grow from tiny seeds. Is it any wonder that from a tiny seed a child picks up the nature of its life and carries that nature on and on?

It was the same when I raised our daughters, only I did not notice it because of the everyday contact I had with them. I thought most of our similarities and gestures were due to our home environment. I was wrong. Much of it is in our genes.

I am astounded at how much biology shapes who we are. Nevertheless, I still believe environment is extremely important in a child's life. That is where they learn right from wrong and develop the character traits that shape the kind of adults they become. In thinking about "nature vs nurture", I know my son is the fine man that he is today, because he had the best of both.

Mike is devoted to his mother and father, and we too have a wonderful relationship. We are still having fun.

21

WHAT I HAVE LEARNED FROM
THE REUNION MOVEMENT

A few months after Mike found me, I realized that I needed to talk to someone about my conflicting emotions. I had heard about Adoptees' Liberty Movement Association (ALMA) and knew there was a chapter in Sacramento, not far from my home. ALMA is a search and support organization for adult adoptees, birth-parents of adoptees, as well as siblings and others who have been separated from their families.

When I first attended meetings in Sacramento I found a safe place to talk openly about my feelings with other birthmothers. I learned that the world of adoption is a very complex one, and that what I was feeling was normal.

When I attended my first ALMA conference, it was celebrating twenty-five years of ALMA's Registry Reunions. Many adopted adult children were still searching and had been for years. Most of the attendees were female, but there were several men as well, birth-fathers and adoptees.

There was one older gentleman who really stood out. I

noticed him and thought he might be a found grandfather or something. When he was introduced to the audience by Florence Fisher, the founder of ALMA, my loud gasp was noticed by all those sitting around me. I started crying.

The man—now in his nineties—was my attorney, Philip Adams.

Hearing his name and seeing him immediately took me back to 1948, sitting in his office, giving my child away. It became real again. It really happened.

I learned that Philip Adams had handled many adoptions and was now doing for all adoptees what he had done for my son. Many of the adoptees he had placed with families were in attendance. One woman, in her forties, who had been searching for some time, tearfully ran over to Philip Adams. He asked for her name and he immediately made an appointment with her for the following week to give her her file.

Later, she was still sobbing and knowing I was a birth-mother, it seemed natural to hold her in my arms. Her sobs were the sobs of a child, filled with joy, sorrow and relief, a child who was still looking for her mommy.

After I became a volunteer for ALMA, I learned that the emotional impact of searching never ends. My role was that of a "happy" found birth-mother, to reassure adoptees that there are birthmothers happy to be found. It worked. I was able to help adoptees during their search just by listening to their fears. Their biggest concern, I learned, was the fear of rejection, and that can be paralyzing. Actual rejection is devastating.

Attending AAC (American Adoption Congress) conferences, I have met more than a few adoptees who have found their birth-mother and were rejected by them. This group of thirty-somethings told me their stories. I could see the pain they were feeling but I didn't know what to say to ease that pain.

I noticed they had all become volunteers for ALMA. I

suppose it is the only source available to them to communicate with other adoptees enduring the same pain. My heart went out to them. They have had good lives, with good adoptive parents, but still something very big is missing.

I advised them not to give up. Being a birth-mother myself, I tell them that their birth-mothers are human and are living with a very traumatic event in their lives. Maybe their current living situation is such that they cannot reveal their secret, and they cannot deal with their exposure at this time.

I suggested that they send polite greeting cards and casual notes, keeping their birth-mothers informed about what they are doing with their lives. Make no demands. I reminded them that they are young and there is time for things to change.

I recommended talking into a tape recorder or writing letters to their birth-mothers, expressing their deep feelings, even telling the birth-mother how angry they feel about being rejected, but not mailing those letters or tapes.

"Just get it out of you. But don't give up," I advised. There should be research on the long-term effect on adoptees who are rejected by their birthmothers. The need is great.

Another group of adoptees who found their birth-mothers were troubled after their reunion. Although they had established a relationship, they felt that the birth-mother was not being truthful with them about the facts of their background story.

I am convinced that every adoptee, when reunited with the birth-parent, has a deep need for the truth about the reason they were placed for adoption. It's the question they have been asking themselves—why?—for as long as they can remember. They have a right to know the truth, no matter how painful the facts are for the birth-parent—or for the adoptee.

The birth-mothers of my generation find it difficult to realize what we did to our children, even though we thought we were doing the right thing. We simply had no idea to whom we were giving our child. Being young, ignorant, and in trouble, we listened to the experts and believed that those who would adopt our child *had* to be wonderful people.

With society looking down on us, and the terrible way we felt about ourselves, we knew our place. We *believed* that the adoptive parents were better than we were. They had money and position to provide the kind of life for our babies that we would never be able to do. Everything, we were told, was going to be "peaches and cream," and we believed it.

Once again, I was thankful that my ignorance protected me from knowing what could have happened to my child. I can't thank God enough that my son had a good life with wonderful loving parents.

I will be eternally grateful that Mike's parents provided a warm, loving home for him and made him the fine decent human being he is today. He is their son and he loves them very much.

It wasn't until attending conferences and talking to adoptees that I heard some of the horror stories about their lives. Thank God, Mike was not mistreated, I don't know how I would have coped with that knowledge.

It is important to stress that *most* adoptions work out well. The adoptees have good lives, good parents, healthy minds, love their parents deeply, but still want to know where they came from and who they are.

Because of sealed birth records, I have witnessed the anguish of adoptees and birth-parents who have no hope of reuniting with each other.

I find it hard to understand how so many in today's society still believe that adoptees have no rights. Why shouldn't adoptees have access to their birth family's medical history? Why are they discriminated against?

The powers that be say birth-mothers should be protected from exposure, from having their lives disrupted by the adoptee. Those same people claim that the adoptee should be protected from the shame of their "illegitimate" heritage.

However, statistics show ninety percent of birth-mothers accept their children, are thrilled to learn they are alive and well, and are anxious for a reunion.

The adopted children had no choice about being taken away from their biological family as infants and given to another family, yet now as adults they are denied access to their own birth records.

It is the ultimate insult to be the only citizens in the United States without the power to decide for themselves about access to their origins.

Adult adoptees should be allowed to see their birth records, to be able to answer the questions they have had all of their lives: "Who am I? Where did I come from? Where did I get this red hair? Why can't I seem to connect with anyone? Where do I belong?" Those are the questions I heard over and over while attending meetings and conferences.

I have met many wonderful women, other birth-mothers, adoptive mothers and adoptees, from all walks of life. We have learned that adoption is a lifelong experience for all of us.

In one of our sessions, while sitting in a circle with other birth-mothers and listening to their experiences during pregnancy, I realized I had been treated well during my time at St. Elizabeth's. Then I recalled something a friend had told me, a retired nurse I met after my reunion with Mike. She knew my story and that I was writing this book. She mentioned she had recently had dinner with an old acquaintance who was a doctor that had interned at St. Mary's Hospital in San Francisco, a block or two from St. Elizabeth's.

She told him about me and that I'd had my baby at St. Elizabeth's. The doctor told her that he had delivered several babies at St. Elizabeth's Foundling Home, as he called it, around the same time that I had been there. He told my friend that he had always been amazed that the young birth-mothers at St. Elizabeth's had always been ready to deliver when he arrived.

He went on to say that he felt sorry for the young mothers and that the nuns must have really manipulated and massaged the mothers to the point that the delivery was immediate. The mothers, being unconscious with ether, were not able to help the nuns during the procedure at all.

I simply have no memory of even entering the delivery room. Hearing what the doctor had told my friend, I tried to remember as much as I could. But I was amazed again by yet another affirmation that it had all really happened. I do remember that I was never examined, not even once, by anyone. Not by a doctor, a nurse or a nun, even though I was eight months pregnant when I arrived there.

What if my baby had been in the wrong position during delivery? How did anyone know that my delivery would be normal? My child could have faced danger without an examination. By comparison, before each of my daughters was born, I went to my doctor every week during my eighth month of pregnancy.

Why does this make me angry now? Being pregnant and unmarried, I had felt like a criminal in 1947. And criminals have no right to complain; criminals have to pay the price for their actions. That was how I felt then. My treatment at St. Elizabeth's, however, had been very good compared to that of many of the other birth-mothers who sat in our group at that conference.

What I came away with from that conference is the belief that birth-mothers and adoptees in reunion have a need for a loving relationship with each other, even those adoptees with wonderful adoptive parents. I met adoptive mothers at conferences who had helped their child search for the birth-parents and were supportive of their reunion. These adoptive mothers were cheered by everyone.

The conferences I attended were an eye-opening experience for me. I was able to talk to many people and learned that as time goes on in this reunion process, more research is being conducted. We all have a hunger and a need to know more.

Society has changed so much over the years. Today, being a birth-mother carries less of a stigma in most circles. We can openly discuss our stories. I'm even writing a book about it, which would not have been the case as late as the 1960's.

Women who could not have children also had a very difficult time in the society of 1947. Knowing how much they wanted children, it must have been painful whenever people would ask, "When are you going to have a baby?"

Some people of that era even thought such couples were selfish and didn't want the responsibility of raising children. Society and relatives were relentless to these couples—being childless carried a stigma. Women and men were made to feel like failures.

Who was to be blamed? The husband or the wife? Both? Or no one? The solution, for many, was adoption.

The decision to adopt a child is a major one. Adoptive couples must meet rigorous requirements before they are allowed to adopt.

When a child searches for his birth-mother or birth-father, the adoptive parents are often reminded of the stigma and the sense of failure that society once put on them.

I can understand how the adoptive mother and father could be fearful of losing their child, but from what I've read and learned through ALMA, most adoptees, after searching and reuniting with a birth-parent, still love their adoptive parents. The adopted child knows the real parents are the ones who gave that child all the love he or she needed while growing up.

The adoptive parents need to trust their children and know that the search is to find their roots and not to take away any of the love they have for their adoptive parents.

Reading all I can on this subject, I find myself wishing someone would find a better name for mothers like me. The term birth-mother makes me think and feel as if I were part of a large group of women who simply produced and provided babies for the baby factory to be deposited for adoption.

It sounds so cold and unfeeling, like the term surrogate mother. It happened to me and does not describe me in the least. I wasn't any of the things that people of my generation called us, or thought of us. I wasn't a tramp, whore, or prostitute. Even less offensive terms such as promiscuous, loose, fast, or immoral didn't describe me. I wasn't even sexy.

I was simply a young girl who fell in love with a cad. This man lied when he asked me to marry him. This country had many thousands of such men back then and there were many thousands of women like me, young, gullible and innocent who succumbed to the romantic charms of more experienced, self-centered men.

Every one of those thousands of women had to work through the heartache of being used, rejected, jilted, ashamed and feeling unclean.

To find yourself in this position is unreal. Humiliation is the word that sums it up best. Then it hits you: What am I going to do?

I can't believe that we all just decided to go to the baby factory and deposit a baby, which is how the term birth-mother makes *me* feel. The decision to let your child go for adoption is one of life's major, most painful, deeply agonizing decisions, and it is made with unselfish love.

It is an everlasting loss. Closed and final.

The shock of Mike's coming back into my life was overwhelming. Reality had to set in for me to realize that he was real. My son and I worked through forty-five years of buried love to reach where we are today. Without the support of the people in the adoption movement, this would have been much more difficult.

We both know and appreciate how lucky we are.

22

AN EVERLASTING GIFT
FROM HEAVEN

M ike and I have been able to visit each other many times over the past years, but still had only that one hour alone until recently. Somehow I managed to have a long leisurely lunch alone with him while visiting a cousin who lives near Mike. It was fun looking at each other without others watching us. We joked about it and wondered if that would ever change. We were very comfortable and as usual time flew by.

Fortunately Chuck and I live only two hours away from Mike and Linda and despite their busy work schedules, we manage to visit them.

I hope someday to be able to talk to him for as long as it takes to know everything I can know about him. Our relationship has grown to a deep mother and child love for each other, the same love I have for my daughters, Susan and Linda.

We have talked about Susan many times, about her life and what kind of a person she was. I wanted Mike to know about his sisters. So I told him some stories about their childhood and how adventurous they had been. Susan and Linda were very close, making it all the more difficult for Linda when Susan died.

I also told Mike many things about my mother. I definitely wanted him to know that even though she had left me alone in that scary flophouse, she was a good person and a good mother to me.

Mike has told me many times, "My one regret is that I missed meeting my grandmother and especially my sister Susan." To this day, we both strongly feel that Susan had played a big role in Mike's finding me—all directed from Heaven.

I will be eternally grateful that Mike's parents provided a warm, loving home for him and helped make him the fine decent human being he is today. He is their son and he loves them very much. Where would he be without them? Who would he be without them? Thank God he was placed in the arms of the wonderful man who would be his father when he was four months old. Mike is the son of a very loving couple who devoted their life to him.

Where would I be without my wonderful husband Chuck? Thank God I had told him about having a child before he asked me to marry him. Watching him with Mike and knowing he genuinely feels Mike is his stepson fills me with everlasting joy. But it's even more than that.

There are a number of things in Mike's background and Chuck's that are similar. Mike's Dad was in the Navy, Chuck was in the Marines. Mike was a policeman, so was Chuck. Both men are fathers of two beautiful daughters. The fact that they seem to have a similar philosophy of life and respect for each other is another blessing.

I wonder what life would be like without Chuck's understanding and support. He has told me he understands my role as a birth-mother, and that Mike and I, not having a history, had a lot of catching up to do. In this situation of awkward moments, Chuck was and still is there for me. We have been a great team and agree on all the important things in life. Both of us know and appreciate how precious our family is.

Even though I have come a long way through this process, I know that for the rest of my life I will regret the fact that I gave my son away. I know I cannot rewrite history, so I still have to deal with my heart telling me that I should have found a way to keep him. Just knowing he is alive and well, though, is more than I could have ever hoped for.

Mike always says, "Thanks for being there," and he knows that I am. Now, I can say, "Thanks for finding me," with confidence that he will never go away.

This wonderful gift from Heaven has been so glorious and joyous that I'm grateful I have had the experience. We are still having fun.

I couldn't ask for anything better.

AFTERWORD

MIKE'S STORY:
FINDING CONTENTMENT
AND WHOLENESS

"What took you so long?" Philip Adams asked over the phone. I couldn't believe that he was still practicing law, in the same old building in downtown San Francisco, forty-five years after he arranged my adoption. This guy had to be in his 90s (88, in fact). He sounded like he was enjoying this.

"Do you have something in your files about me?" I blurted out the big question.

"Yes," he answered, "I have all the old files in the basement and I do have something in my files about you."

Did he say yes? His words washed over me like a tidal wave, sucking the air out of my lungs, blurring my vision, and making my head pound. After five years of searching, maybe this was it.

"But first," he said, "tell me what you know."

Catching my breath, I replied, "I've got my mother's birth certificate. A Betty Jean Heath. I also have my father's."

I felt proud to have some information about myself already. It seemed like a miracle to be talking to him.

"I'm told you handled my adoption—your name was given me by my parents."

"Which ones?"

This guy went directly to the heart of the matter.

"My adoptive parents," I said, wondering what he would tell me.

"Well, I have your file," he repeated, "but I've got a *Beth* Jean Heath. Not Betty. She was born in Oakland, September 2, 1927."

I was stunned. My mind couldn't grasp the significance of what he'd just said.

"Hello, are you still there . . . ?"

"Are you sure that's her name?" I choked out.

"Well, name's on the back . . . Beth Heath, 1948. She's a real looker, too. I have a picture of her and she's holding a baby. Is that you?"

"What?"

A picture of my birth-mother? With me! It couldn't be. Mom and Dad said they'd never met her and that she never saw me.

For a moment I thought he had the wrong lady, and I was about to tell him so when it hit me: he couldn't be wrong. He was looking at my file, the very one he put together forty-five years earlier. I was the one with the wrong information. I'd been looking for the wrong lady for five years.

From the earliest of my recollections, I'd known I was adopted. Even when I didn't understand the term, my parents simply ingrained in me the special love it meant by being "picked."

"Other parents had to take what they got. We got to pick you," was the way I most remember it, and proudly repeated it to my playmates.

For a time, I've been struggling with the way it is necessary to distinguish between my birth-mother and my adoptive parents in telling my story.

Beth is my mother, the lady who gave me life—a very courageous act at a time when to do so meant lifelong pain and humiliation.

Mom is . . . well, Mom. She was at the Little League games, the Boy Scout meetings, helping with the homework, agonizing over my first time behind the wheel, my first date, feeling fear every time I headed to the beach with the surfboard on the roof-rack at 6 a.m.

I have tried to identify these people as my adoptive-mother, adoptive-father, adoptive-parents. I can't. No more than I could stand to be referred to as "an adopted-son." She's my Mom. He's my Dad. And I'm their son. No hyphens. They were always there.

While acceptable in the world of adoption and the congress of people involved in the mind-set of search, discovery and awakening, such terms can't be used in reference to the people who love, cherish and protect the children they take to their hearts, minds and souls.

Every day I am grateful for the way they've helped to shape and mold the ethic of the person I am. The knowledge that I was born in San Francisco to "a nice girl who got in trouble" was all I needed, I guess. It satisfied my curiosity for many years.

Childhood was a series of new places to live none near San Francisco. My father, a Pearl Harbor survivor (U.S.S. *West Virginia*), served in the Navy for thirty years. Every two years or so, we found ourselves in a new place to live—generally on one coast or the other. San Diego, Great Lakes, Washington, DC, my favorites. Guam was in there somewhere, too. So was Texas.

San Diego is where I stopped. High school, college, career and marriage. The things that usually make one stop. Oh, and kids, too.

It wasn't until I returned to Northern California years later that the idea of actually running into the woman who gave me life became a possibility. I was working for a radio station in Grass Valley-Nevada City in 1978. I had the perfect job in the perfect place (the Sierra Nevada foothills) and still, there was something missing.

And it wasn't until I met Linda, the lady who would become my second wife, that, in detailing my life story, I began to recognize what I might have been searching for.

Linda was and is all-consuming. Her enthusiasm for life, her courage to take on any challenge, her loyalty to my psychological needs and to me, all came together in one magnificent package. It was she that first suggested, "Let's find her."

"Who?"

"Your real mother."

Linda drove and I looked, as we toured the streets of San Francisco. Silly as that seems, it's true. I stared at everyone I saw in that city, looking to find someone with a resemblance.

There are a lot of people in San Francisco—like finding a needle in a haystack, I thought. On one trip I even looked up the name of the attorney that my parents gave me on the day of my first marriage. I had carried it ever since. It was written on a slip of paper, along with the name of my birth-mother.

Betty Jean Heath.

Philip Adams.

Suddenly, the idea of finding out more became real, but even with Linda's urging I hesitated. The idea was overwhelming.

In the fall of 1987, I was hired as news director at my small town's only radio station. Life was good, things were on the upswing. Linda was finding success in the dog show world and I was making my mark on the community. We were on our way.

I hadn't been at the station a month when I got a call from Linda.

"Guess what I just did?" she chirped.

"What now?"

"I just sent away for a copy of your birth certificate."

"Why? I have that."

"Well, I want to see if there's anything on it about your real mother. It's a start."

Linda was incensed when she looked at the birth certificate she received.

"It's a lie. A public record that purposely lies about something so important as a birth!"

It showed my adoptive parents as being my natural ones. I'd known this because my parents proudly told me it did. Over the next five years, I sent away for other birth records and as much information as I could find.

Having the name Betty Jean Heath, I thought Betty had to be short for Elizabeth, so after many letters and phone calls to the Bureau of Vital Statistics, I found a birth certificate for Elizabeth Jean Heath, born twenty years before me. My birth-mother?

Birth certificates contain a wealth of information. Parents' names, mother's maiden name, siblings, if any, address at the time of birth—the list goes on, but each bit of information hits like a hammer blow. Each requires time to be digested.

It was like opening a door an inch at a time, each giving just a hint of the whole picture, yet each bit of knowledge exploding across the mind like a thunderbolt. It would take weeks for the excitement to subside after discovering a new fragment of the fabric of my life. Like coming off a big high, great while it lasted, but scary, too: "Stop! I know all I want to know."

I went around in circles with all this in my head for too long, until my daughters sat me down and told me they also wanted to know. By that time, Kim and Seana were young women in college, each studying the healthcare-education field. They knew the importance of family history as it relates to health issues and so they said, "If you want to find out about her, Dad, we'll do whatever we can to help." That is when I gave myself permission to really make it happen.

First Linda; now my daughters. The three most important people in my life, all focused on helping me in this quest.

Now it was time to play the "trump card." That card I'd been afraid to play all through the years because it was my last hope. An unwanted end to the fantasy of actually finding my birth-mother. That slip of paper with the lawyer's name, Philip Adams.

I had no choice. After weeks of sleepless nights, I finally picked up the phone. It wasn't until I actually spoke to Philip Adams that I discovered I had been searching for the wrong woman all this time. Even more surprising, when he handed me my file it revealed that I was not born at St. Mary's Hospital as I had been told. When I learned I was born at St. Elizabeth's Home for Unwed Mothers, Linda and I drove by it and I was very impressed.

Little did I know then how soon it would be before I was to wrap up one of the most emotionally challenging, frustrating and fulfilling chapters of my life. Nor did I know of the wonderful things that were about to happen to me, or about the life and the love and the lady who is now my best friend.

But, without Chuck, this would have been a very different story, because it soon became apparent that if there is an angel living on this earth, his name is Chuck Kane.

It was he I most feared.

Did he know about me? Probably not. How was I to reach out to this as yet unknown lady, identify myself as the son she gave birth to forty-five years earlier, and not totally disrupt her life—the last thing I wanted—if her husband did not know about me?

Fortunately, he did. And, while I went looking for a "Mother," because of the size of this man's heart, and the love he holds for his wife, I also ended up finding a "very special stepfather."

Never once in all the time since the reunion have I felt anything but love and excitement from this gentlest of giants. Standing six feet, six inches tall, he fills a room with his presence, personality and the adoration he holds for his bride. I admire him very much, and I thank him in my prayers every day.

When I began this quest for my mother, my intent was far different than when it ended. I only wanted to find out who she was. I never intended to make contact. I wanted to find a family tree—not a whole new family. My parents and I are very close, always have been and continue to be. I just wanted to fill in the blanks, put names on the empty branches of that tree, so to speak.

I was also curious to know what happened to her after my birth. Maybe get a picture of her somehow. Was she alive? Did I have any siblings? I'd always thought I wanted some. What I found was two sisters—one a spiritual sister, the other a fantastic lady I've come to admire and love for her intelligence, charm and especially for the compassion she holds for everyone in her world.

And it only recently occurred to me that all of this has been the result of Susan, the sister I never met, who died in 1985. The lady who most resembles my daughter, Kim. The sister who, before her illness, told her cousin she was going to "find" me.

She is the key to all that has happened since. I feel her soft touch as I write these words. I miss her and I never even knew her. I know in my heart that it was she who kept whispering in my ear, "Find mother. She needs you."

. . . Yes, my life is filled with angels.

The first two organizations provide a national registry for persons seeking someone lost to them by adoption.

Adoptees' Liberty Movement Association (ALMA)
P.O. Box 727
Radio City Station
New York, NY 10101-0727
(212) 581-1568

International Soundex Reunion Registry
P.O. Box 2312
Carson City, NV 10021
(707) 882-7755

American Adoption Congress (AAC)
100 Connecticut Avenue, NW Suite 9
Washington, D.C. 20036
1-800-274-6736

The AAC is an umbrella organization that publishes a newsletter and sponsors regional and national conferences. The AAC is active in Adoption Reform.

Post Adoption Center for Education and Research (PACER)
P.O. Box 743
Corte Madera, CA 94976-0743
(925) 935-6622

Concerned United Birthparents (CUB)
2000 Walker Street
Des Moines, IA 50317
(515) 263-9558

Bastard Nation
12865 NE 85th Street
Suite 179
Kirkland, WA 98033
Website: http://www.bastards.org/

Titles Published by Aslan

PUBLISHING

The Candida Control
Cookbook What You
Should Know And What
You Should Eat To
Manage Yeast Infections
by Gail Burton
$13.95
ISBN 0-944031-67-6

Gentle Roads To Survival:
Making Self-Healing Choices
in Difficult Circumstances
by Andre Auw Ph.D.
$10.95
ISBN 0-944031-18-8

The Gift of Wounding:
Finding Hope & Heart
in Challenging
Circumstances
by Andre Auw Ph.D.
$13.95
ISBN 0-944031-79-X

How Loving Couples Fight:
12 Essential Tools for
Working Through the Hurt
by James L Creighton Ph.D.
$16.95
ISBN 0-944031-71-4

Intuition Workout: A
Practical Guide To
Discovering & Developing
Your Inner Knowing
by Nancy Rosanoff
$12.95
ISBN 0-944031-14-5

The Joyful Child:
A Sourcebook of Activities
and Ideas for Releasing
Children's Natural Joy
by Peggy Jenkins Ph.D.
$16.95
ISBN 0-944031-66-8

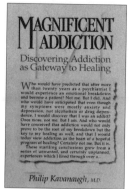

Lovers For Life: Creating Lasting Passion, Trust and True Partnership by Daniel Ellenberg Ph.D. & Judith Bell M.S., MFCC
$16.95
ISBN 0-944031-61-7

Magnificent Addiction: Discovering Addiction as Gateway to Healing by Philip R. Kavanaugh, M.D.
$14.95
ISBN 0-944031-36-6

More Than Just Sex: A Committed Couples Guide to Keeping Relationships Lively, Intimate & Gratifying by Daniel Beaver M.S., MFCC
$12.95
ISBN0-944031-35-8

Mind, Music & Imagery: Unlocking the Treasures of Your Mind by Stephanie Merritt
$13.95
ISBN 0-944031-62-5

New Woman Manager: 50 Fast & Savvy Solutions for Executive Excellence by Sharon Lamhut Willen
$14.95
ISBN 0-944031-11-0

The Motion Picture Prescription Watch This Movie and Call Me in The Morning: 200 Movies to help you heal life's problems by Gary Solomon Ph.D. "The Movie Doctor "
$12.95
ISBN 0-944031-27-7

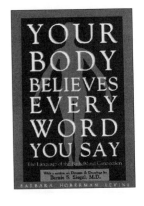

Solstice Evergreen: The History, Folklore & Origins of the Christmas Tree
2nd ed by Sheryl Karas
$14.95
ISBN 0-944031-75-7

What Happened to the Prince I Married: Spiritual Healing for a Wounded Relationship
by Sirah Vettese Ph.D.
$14.95
ISBN 0-944031-76-5

Your Body Believes Every Word You Say: The Language of the Body Mind Connection
by Barbara Hoberman Levine $13.95
ISBN 0-944031-07-2

More Aslan Titles

Facing Death, Finding Love: The Healing Power Of Grief & Loss in One Family's Life
by Dawson Church, $10.95; ISBN 0-944031-31-5

If You Want To Be Rich & Happy, Don't Go to School Ensuring Lifetime Security for Yourself & Your Children by Robert Kiyosaki $14.95; ISBN 0-944031-59-5

Lynn Andrews in Conversation with Michael Toms
edited by Hal Zina Bennett, $8.95; ISBN 0-944031-42-0

Argument With An Angel
by Jan Cooper, $11.95; ISBN 0-944031-63-3

To order any of Aslan's titles send a check or money order for the price of the book plus Shipping & Handling

Book Rate $3 for 1st book.; $1.00 for each additional book
First Class $4 for 1st book; $1.50 for each additional book

Send to: ***Aslan Publishing***
2490 Black Rock Turnpike # 342
Fairfield CT 06432

To receive a current catalog: please call (800) 786–5427 or (203) 372–0300
E-mail us at: **info@aslanpublishing.com**
Visit our website at **www.aslanpublishing.com**

Our authors are available for seminars, workshops, and lectures. For further information or to reach a specific author, please call or email Aslan Publishing.